Silver Palaces

AMERICA'S STREAMLINED TRAILERS

Silver Palaces

DOUGLAS KEISTER

Gibbs Smith, Publisher
Salt Lake City

To Life, Liberty, and the Pursuit of Happiness

First Edition
15 14   7 6

Text and photographs © 2004 Douglas Keister

Published by
Gibbs Smith, Publisher
P.O. Box 667
Layton, Utah 84041

1.800.748.5439 orders
www.gibbs-smith.com

Designed and produced by Steve Rachwal
Printed and bound in China

Library of Congress Cataloging-in-Publication Data
Keister, Douglas.
    Silver palaces : America's streamlined trailers / Douglas Keister.–1st ed.
        p. cm.
Includes bibliographical references.
ISBN 1-58685-352-5
1. Travel trailers — United States. I. Title.
TL297.K3823 2004
629.226–dc22
                            2004005054

Contents

Foreword: *Streamlining*

by Arrol Gellner, syndicated columnist of Architext

STREAMLINING: FUNCTION, FORM, FASHION

Nowadays we take it for granted that an object's appearance should reflect its function. Yet this is a relatively modern conceit. For the first hundred years following the Industrial Revolution, function and appearance were treated as coexistent yet separate entities. A cookstove's functionality was one thing; its decoration was quite another. Mass-produced products were reflexively embellished with a wide variety of historical motifs having no connection with their purpose. Even a modern object free of historical precedent, such as a stationary steam engine, might be decorated with antique motifs, whether Gothic, Renaissance, or Egyptian.

A LAST LOOK BACK

In the late nineteenth century, the Arts and Crafts movement arose largely to decry the application of such arbitrary ornament to mass-produced products. Instead, it espoused a more honest decorative vocabulary growing out of the object's construction — an ideal harking back to the medieval craftsmanship of preindustrial times. A piece of wooden furniture, for example, might express its pegged or dovetailed connections rather than having its structure concealed and overlaid with historical motifs. Architecture was likewise expected to make forthright use of natural materials that did not attempt to imitate other finishes. While the Arts and Crafts movement revolutionized domestic design, it had less impact on industrial design. Ultimately, economic forces, not philosophical ones, would shape the aesthetic of manufactured products.

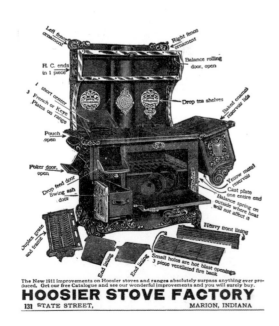

The New 1911 improvements on Hoosier stoves and ranges absolutely surpass anything ever produced. Get our free Catalogue and see our wonderful improvements and you will surely buy.

HOOSIER STOVE FACTORY
131 STATE STREET,   MARION, INDIANA

early 1930s. Early mass-produced automobiles, too, began moving away from applied decoration by the early teens. While the interiors of custom-built touring cars still owed more to an Edwardian parlor than to any mechanical aesthetic—some examples boasted inlaid wood paneling, brocade upholstery, and flower vases—affordable, mass-produced automobiles necessarily became much more spartan. The trend was epitomized by the stark lines of the Model T Ford, which could famously be had in any color as long as it was black. In lieu of superficial decoration, motorcars gradually became more expressive of their engineering. Functional requirements such as engine placement and passenger space dictated their basic form, from which a new and unprecedented aesthetic began to develop. The larger

AESTHETICS MEETS ECONOMICS

Steam locomotives were among the earliest industrial objects to dispense with applied decoration. Since the 1840s, locomotive builders had lavished their products with pinstriping, brass appliqués, multicolor paint schemes, and other nonessential embellishments. However, a focus on efficiency and profit soon led the nation's railroads to do away with such frivolity. By the 1880s, locomotives had taken on the dark, drab, yet purposeful appearance they would retain until the

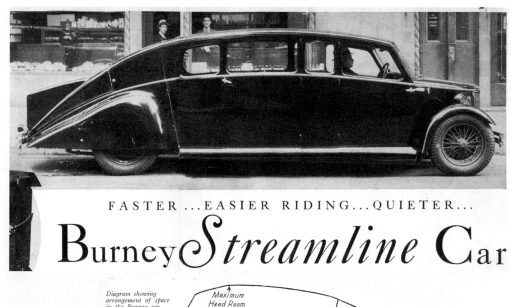

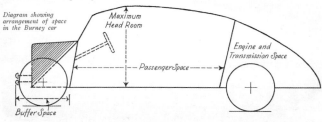

FASTER...EASIER RIDING...QUIETER...

Burney *Streamline* Car

Diagram showing arrangement of space in the Burney car

Maximum Head Room

Engine and Transmission Space

Passenger Space

Buffer Space

INSPIRATION DESCENDS ON WINGS

and more powerful engines offered on costlier makes, for example, were reflected in extended hoods and longer wheelbases — attributes that would come to symbolize automotive power and prestige for the next fifty years. Alas, automotive engineers sometimes proved inadequate to the task of designing beautiful shapes based on technical needs alone, as the many stodgy vehicle designs of the early twenties will testify. Consequently, by the middle of the decade, both Ford and General Motors had organized specialized groups to deal specifically with automotive aesthetics. The 1927 LaSalle was among the first mass-produced efforts of these so-called "stylists."

Around the same time stylists arrived, the technologically salient aircraft industry began to influence industrial designers. Aircraft forms, their designs aided by wind tunnel tests, had steadily become sleeker and more aerodynamic, and these exciting new shapes would soon influence mass-produced products of all kinds. In 1901, the Wright brothers had constructed the first wind tunnel to evaluate the lift of various wing profiles. It was a modest affair, sixteen inches square by about six feet long, but it laid the groundwork for all subsequent aerodynamic testing. In 1917, aircraft pioneer Glenn Curtiss built a much larger, seven-foot-diameter tunnel in Hempstead, New York. That same year, the first

mass-produced all-metal airframe design appeared in the guise of the Junkers J.4; portentously, the German fighter was sheathed in Duralumin, an alloy one-third the weight of steel. While wood-and-canvas aircraft designs would linger for decades, the course of modern aviation had already been set. In 1921, the U.S. government completed the first in a succession of wind tunnels at its airfield in Langley, Virginia. The 1920s and early '30s brought continual refinement in aerodynamics, along with the gradual adoption of modern fundamentals such as the cantilevered monoplane wing and stressed-skin construction. In 1933, the Italian Macchi-72 seaplane broke the aircraft speed record with a 423-mile-per-hour run over Lake Garda, aided by its remarkably sleek fuselage. In the United States, the combination of lightweight, all-metal monoplane designs and increasingly sophisticated aerodynamic testing resulted in breathtaking streamlined aircraft such as the twin-engined Douglas Air Liner and the Lockheed Electra.

A NEW INDUSTRIAL IDEAL

The fact that such beautiful forms were generated by technical efficiency rather than by some arbitrary aesthetic convinced many industrial designers that streamlining held the key to truly modern forms. By the early 1930s, streamlined aircraft design was already influencing the auto industry. Chrysler Corporation was first to take the

streamlining plunge with its Airflow models of 1934, whose unconventional silhouette arose from the discovery that most cars offered less wind resistance when moving backwards. The Airflow's design eschewed the bolt-upright radiator and timidly raked windshield typical of the period, instead emulating the sloping trunk lid and softly-rounded contours found at the rear of most cars. Although the Airflow was probably too radical for the mainstream market — its sales were disappointing — there was no turning back. Within a few years, all American automakers had adopted some form of streamlined styling. In the travel trailer industry, a few hardy pioneers followed suit. The most notable was William Hawley Bowlus, who introduced his ultralight, aircraft-based Road Chief, the forefather of the Airstream and all other "silver palaces," in 1934. That story will

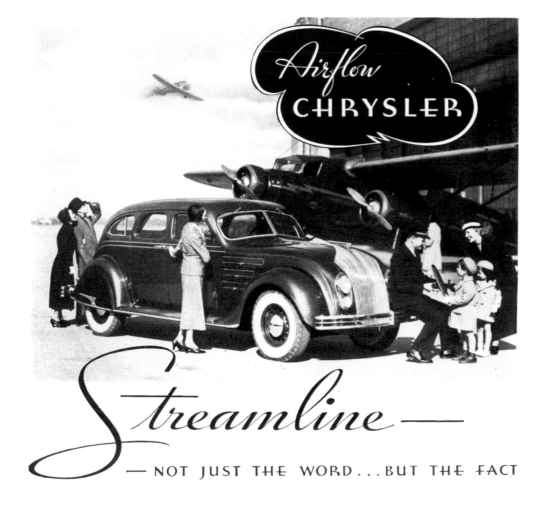

Airflow
CHRYSLER

Streamline —
— NOT JUST THE WORD...BUT THE FACT

SEE UNION PACIFIC'S LATEST HIGH-SPEED STREAMLINE TRAIN

NEW 6 CAR TRAIN WITH 3 PULLMAN SLEEPING CARS

ON EXHIBIT CINCINNATI

WEDNESDAY, NOVEMBER 14 – 9:30 A.M. – 9 P.M.

Union Station - Track 12

follow in "Silver Genesis." Meanwhile, American railroads once again strove to outdo each other as they had a century earlier, this time with flashy streamlined locomotives styled by high-profile industrial designers. Among these were Raymond Loewy's sleek GG-1 electric locomotives for the Pennsylvania Railroad, introduced in 1934, and Henry Dreyfus's bullet-nosed J3 steam locomotives for the New York Central, circa 1937. The arrival of diesel-electric passenger locomotives, whose running gear could be easily concealed beneath shrouding, spurred the streamlining trend. First among these was the Chicago, Burlington & Quincy's speed-record-setting Pioneer Zephyr and the Union Pacific's M-10001, both dating from 1934. Since there was little technical gain in locomotive streamlining, such designs enhanced public relations more than they did efficiency. Streamlining had become an emblem of modernity, and by the late 1930s, curvacious housings embossed with a few horizontal "speedlines" to suggest motion were being even less plausibly applied to such products as typewriters, toasters, and mimeograph machines. Even modern architecture briefly flirted with fashionable curves and speed-lines in the Art Deco–based variant

TOASTMASTER *Toaster*

REG. U.S. PAT. OFF.

AUTOMATIC POP-UP TYPE

we now call Streamline Moderne. Ironically, since the effectiveness of a wringer washer or a roasting pan hardly depended on its moving smoothly through the air, this trend was the farthest thing from form expressing function. The erstwhile science of streamlining had been hijacked by fashion to become little more than a novel form of decoration. In 1939, the New York World's Fair presented the streamlining craze at its exuberant apogee. Most every new product displayed, from motorcars to mixers, seemed poised to momentarily become airborne. With the Great War and the depression both blessedly fading memories, this was an age of unbridled optimism in things American. Streamlining epitomized that bold new assurance: it bespoke a nation's running leap into the future.

Silver Genesis

The genesis of the streamlined aluminum trailer lies with the story of William Hawley Bowlus (1886–1967). Before the introduction of the Bowlus Road Chief trailer in 1934, streamlining in the trailer industry was limited to wood-and-painted-canvas trailers. The most noted manufacturer was Glenn Curtiss, who made fifth-wheel trailers with a painted fabric skin stretched over a wood frame. Curtiss made his imprint in the aerodynamic world by manufacturing airplanes and later merged with the Wright brothers to form the Curtiss-Wright Corporation. Curtiss's trailers, which he called Aerocars, were largely a plaything of the wealthy, although a number of them were built for commercial uses, including stylish containers for traveling salesmen's wares, ambulances, and funeral limousines. Other manufacturers made trailers that they called streamlined, but their creations had plywood or Masonite skin and looked more like a huge egg balanced on wheels than a zoomy streamlined trailer.

CURTISS AEROCAR

This 1936 Curtiss Aerocar is a testament to streamlining. In addition to its streamlined shape, it sports skirted rear wheels with "speed line" emblems. The equally rakish tow car is a 1934 Hudson coupe. The exterior of the trailer is painted fabric applied to a wood frame. The trailer and car, owned by Vince Martinico/Auburn Trailer Collection, were photographed in Newcastle, California.

TO MY BOWLUS ROAD CHIEF
S. W. Sensiba

Fervent wish was mine to see
  Springtime bloom of desert sand,—
Viewing all of Nature's lore
  In her glorious wonderland.

Highways lure to peaks of snow,
  Rugged pines, and trouting stream;
And the roar of breaking wave
  Stencils out another dream.

Now I have a graceful tube
  Wrought of steel and light dural
Groomed to pierce resistant air
  With an ease no words can tell.

Comfort makes a happy home
  As we travel here and there.
Pull the gang plank, wave adieu!
  Road Chief, "Bowl-us" anywhere!

Written by Permission of Dr. S. W. Sensiba

BOWLUS TELLER
COMPANY

13785 Paxton Avenue   Telephone San Fernando 169
            SAN FERNANDO, CALIFORNIA

BOWLUS-TELLER MANUFACTURING COMPANY
SAN FERNANDO, CALIFORNIA

BOWLUS ROAD CHIEF

A Bowlus brochure shows a Bowlus Road Chief in the California desert. On the back of the brochure is an outdoorsy poem, "To My Bowlus Road Chief," written by Dr. S. W. Sensiba. Courtesy Leo and Marlys Keoshian Collection.

Like his streamlining counterpart Glenn Curtiss, Hawley Bowlus got his start in the aviation industry. Bowlus was the shop foreman for an airplane manufacturer in San Diego named Ryan Airlines. One day in early 1927 Ryan Airlines got a telegram: "CAN YOU CONSTRUCT WHIRLWIND ENGINE PLANE CAPABLE OF FLYING NONSTOP BETWEEN NEW YORK AND PARIS STOP IF SO PLEASE STATE COST AND DELIVERY DATE." That telegram was from a young aviator named Charles Lindbergh. The rest, as they say, is history. Bowlus's crew started building the Ryan NYP (New York–Paris) *Spirit of Saint Louis* on February 28, 1927, and sixty days later, it was ready to fly. The plane was then shipped to New York and on May 20, 1927, Charles Lindbergh took off from New York. He landed twenty-seven hours later in Paris.

When Lindbergh returned to San Diego after his historic flight, he asked Bowlus what he could do for him and Bowlus's wife, Ruth; in addition to becoming good friends, Lindbergh had stayed at the Bowlus home. Bowlus asked if he could have the plane's spinner (the pointed device at the front of the propeller). Lindbergh gladly gave the couple the spinner, and in the late 1990s Ruth gave the spinner to the National Air and Space Museum.

Bowlus, who had been building gliders since 1910, continued with a stellar career in aviation. His most notable achievements were the construction of a number of sailplanes. In 1930 he built the first U.S.–made high-performance sailplane, which he called the *Albatross,* and in 1932 established a new soaring record by staying aloft for more than nine hours. When Bowlus tested his sailplanes, he often had to spend a considerable amount of time camping out in the desert. During one of those excursions, the proverbial lightbulb must have gone off, because a plan was hatched to build a trailer to stay in during his sailplane tests. This trailer would be based on the aircraft principles he had learned. Soon the Bowlus-duPont Sailplane Company had a subsidiary — the Bowlus-Teller Manufacturing Company — thanks to the financial backing of Jacob Teller.

From 1934 until 1936 Bowlus-Teller produced about 150 trailers in its factory in San Fernando, California. It is unclear if all of the trailer models listed in the brochure were built (there has never been a documented photograph of a model called the Trail-Ur-Boat, which was a clamshell affair consisting of two boats clamped together, gunnel to gunnel). What is clear is that the Bowlus-Teller trailers were the first lightweight streamlined trailers using Duralumin. Bowlus also pioneered the use of monocoque trailers (a type of construction found in airplanes, where the body and frame are integrated into one unit). Bowlus was, understandably, a big promoter of the virtues of streamlining. In fact, in one of his brochures, he claims that, because of some unstated aerodynamic principle, towing a Bowlus-Teller streamlined trailer at speeds more than forty-five miles per hour actually increased the car's mileage. Bowlus does go on to say, "At slow speeds in traffic and on grades this did not hold true, but the increase in gas consumption was in no way abnormal or excessive."

The most popular Bowlus-Teller trailers were the Road Chief models, which came in Standard, De Luxe, and Special Commercial configurations. Road Chiefs came with a two-burner stove, icebox, water tank and pump, kapok-filled leather cushions, and a telephone system that connected to the car (this was before laws that forbade travel in a moving trailer). Available accessories were brakes, safety glass, and a loud speaker that connected to the car's radio.

Bowlus-Teller trailers were truly revolutionary, but with prices ranging from $750 for the diminutive Papoose,

1935 BOWLUS PAPOOSE

Rarest of the rare. This 1935 Bowlus Papoose (only four are known to exist) is a mere 11 feet 6 inches in length, 6 feet wide, 7 feet high, and weighs in at 700 pounds. Like the Road Chief, the Papoose is entered from the fore end. The present owners found it in abysmal condition (it had been painted and had numerous dents and pits) but restored it to pristine condition through hours of toil. The Papoose, owned by Leo and Marlys Keoshian, is towed with a 1934 Packard Coupe Roadster owned by Tom Williams.

to more than $7,500 for the Motor Chief, their offerings were beyond the means of most Americans. By 1936 the company was in bankruptcy. Trailers as revolutionary as the ones designed by William Hawley Bowlus would need someone with the marketing ability of a P. T. Barnum. That task would fall upon a one-time salesman for Bowlus-Teller, who would purchase much of the equipment from the bankrupt company. That person, Wallace "Wally" Byam, subtly reconfigured the Bowlus-Teller trailer and began marketing it under the Airstream name.

1935 BOWLUS PAPOOSE (INTERIOR)

Every square inch is utilized in the Papoose interior. There is a small galley at the entrance (out of view) and the dinette converts into a bed. Four windows, two of which serve as skylights, provide ample illumination. The warm wood paneling gives the Papoose the feel of a very cozy summer cabin. The owners have decorated the trailer with period accessories, including a portrait of New Deal president Franklin D. Roosevelt, 1930s tableware, and the owners' most treasured trailer accessory—a cookbook for trailerites titled Meals on Wheels.

1935 BOWLUS ROAD CHIEF

The rear view of the Bowlus Road Chief accentuates its airplane-like fuselage. Like an airplane, the Bowlus's Duralumin skin was applied over aluminum ribs, yielding a total weight of a mere 1,100 pounds. One major design flaw of the Bowlus was the configuration of the rear cat's-eye windows, which tended to leak. The rear windows of this Bowlus have been covered over to prevent leaks. Seemingly more airplane than trailer, Bowlus-Teller's Road Chief set a new standard in trailer technology. William Hawley Bowlus, a brilliant sailplane designer whose Albatross glider set numerous records for nonpowered flight, put his experience to good use in the Road Chief's design. As has often been the case with pioneering products, however, the Road Chief's advanced design did not translate into strong sales. Bowlus-Teller was out of business by 1936, though its trailer was soon reborn under new auspices. The trailer, owned by Vince Martinico/Auburn Trailer Collection, was photographed in Auburn, California.

1935 BOWLUS ROAD CHIEF (SIDE VIEW)

The side view of the Bowlus Road Chief shows off its fanciful zeppelin-like shape. Hawley Bowlus's decision to have the door on the end of the trailer rather than on the side resulted in a more blunt fore end. The placement of the door and the resultant shape makes the Bowlus one of the easiest trailers to identify. Although the skin on this trailer was in relatively straight condition, it was severely pitted, so the owner decided to paint the trailer with a metallic paint used on Honda cars rather than polish the Duralumin. The trailer, owned by Bob and Marilyn West, was photographed at Rancho Los Alamitos, Long Beach, California.

1935 BOWLUS ROAD CHIEF (INTERIOR)

The Road Chief's lovingly restored interior, austerely paneled in a honey-toned birch, conveys the basic simplicity of Bowlus's conception. The lounge area in the foreground occupies the central portion of the trailer, with the sleeping area tucked into the pointed aft end. A tiny galley, not visible here, flanks the front-mounted entrance door. The diminutive Art Deco–flavored lighting fixtures reflect the architectural fashion of the era.

The Papoose logo was re-created by the owners of the trailer.

The original nameplate appears on the Papoose.

A bevy of beauties lounge in a 1935 Bowlus Road
Chief. The colorized black-and-white photograph
appeared in a 1936 magazine article titled "Hitch
Your Wagon to a Car." The caption reads,
"Commodious interior of a large trailer home. Note
the yacht-like arrangement of the furnishings to
take advantage of every inch of space." Courtesy
Leo and Marlys Keoshian Collection.

1936 BOWLUS ROAD CHIEF

This view aptly illustrates the front-mounted door above the trailer tongue; the galley is just visible within. The unconventional entrance location allowed Bowlus to provide a taller opening and also avoided the complication of placing a door in the trailer's rounded sides. This feature makes the Bowlus easy to identify, since it was the only trailer (other than a few custom one-of-a-kind trailers) that had an end entrance. The 18-foot-3-inch Bowlus Road Chief was restored by Don Mayton and Dean Tryon in 1993-94. The Road Chief is towed with a 1936 Buick Roadmaster four-door sedan with a 320-cubic-inch straight-eight engine. The trailer and car, owned by Don and Carol Mayton, were photographed at Camp Dearborn, Michigan.

The trailer's owner re-created the Bowlus Road Chief logo.

ANOTHER type of streamline trailer of metal construction. Note the front door entrance over the parking stand and the large windows.

1936 BOWLUS ROAD CHIEF (FRONT END)

Despite the awkward location of the entry door, this photograph from 1936 illustrates that the trailer could be accessed without bumping one's head. Side-mounted doors often had warning signs (added by the owner) cautioning about the possibility of contusions. Courtesy of Leo and Marlys Keoshian Collection.

By H. W. MAGEE
PART II

WE are getting ready to live on wheels. The exodus from the American home is under way by a tax-ridden population clamoring for independence and freedom of movement.

That is the astonishing conclusion of no less an authority than Roger W. Babson, statistician and economist. Following an extensive survey, Mr. Babson a few months ago made an amazing prediction.

"Within twenty years," he said, "more than half the population of the United States will be living in automobile trailers."

In other words, if Mr. Babson is right, you have more than an even chance of calling a trailer coach your home within two decades. Uprooting half the people of the country and starting them out in rolling homes within the space of a few years seems preposterous until we take a look at this trailer business—perhaps the fastest growing industry in America today.

Five years ago a trailer coach was a novelty. The man who owned one had no privacy because curious throngs hammered on his door, peeked in his windows and demanded information on costs, upkeep, comfort, ventilation, miles per gallon and a hundred other subjects. That should have been a

BOWLUS-TELLER SALES BROCHURE

A sales brochure for Bowlus-Teller (Teller was a financial partner in the business) shows Hawley Bowlus's wife, Ruth, with the 1934 five-window coupe she used to deliver the trailers. Hawley and Ruth once towed a Bowlus all the way from California to Ohio to deliver it to a customer. Courtesy Leo and Marlys Keoshian Collection.

BOWLUS-TELLER TRAILERS

BOWLUS - TELLER MANUFACTURING CO.

13785 Paxton Avenue   San Fernando 169
SAN FERNANDO, CALIFORNIA

◆

WM. HAWLEY BOWLUS, President & General Manager
JACOB TELLER, Treasurer

◆

BEAUTIFUL	ROOMY
ECONOMICAL	COMFORTABLE
DURABLE	CONVENIENT

"Make Touring a Pleasure"

Patents Pending
Copyright 1935 Bowlus-Teller Mfg. Co.

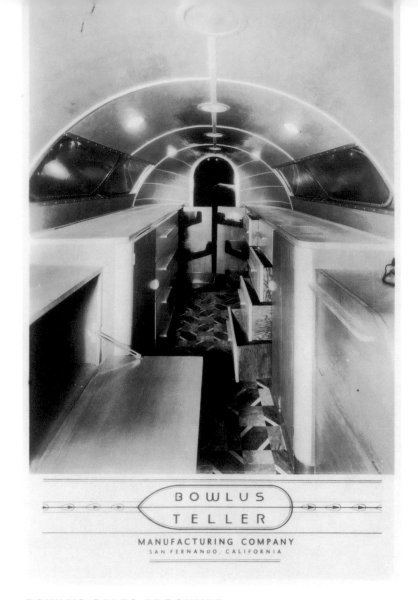

BOWLUS SALES BROCHURE

An illustration from a Bowlus sales brochure shows how the interior could be configured to the customer's needs. Bowlus trailers, as well as other trailers, were popular with traveling salesmen and people who worked in the field, like geologists, archaeologists, and construction workers. Courtesy Leo and Marlys Keoshian Collection.

COMMANDER GATTI AD

Streamlining knew no boundaries in the late 1930s. Bowlus-Teller may have gone bankrupt and upstart Wally Byam may have taken center stage, but others also hitched their trailers to the fashionable streamline star. Streamlined trailers even made it to the "Equatorial Heart of Darkest Africa." This 1938 advertisement for International Trucks describes the preparations for an expedition by well-known Italian explorer Commander Attilio Gatti, who seemed to have the same gift for showmanship as P. T. Barnum and Wally Byam. The advertisement centered on twin streamlined 28-foot Jungle Yachts, designed by one Count Alexis de Sakhnoffsky. The two trailers could be joined together by an accordion-like device to provide a five-room apartment for Mr. and Mrs. Gatti, complete with a full-size bathtub, electric lighting, two bedrooms, and an observation deck. Gatti's expedition was widely covered in magazines and newspapers such as Esquire, **Look** *and the* Saturday Evening Post. *Upon his return, a twenty-page brochure titled "Adventure and Misadventure Behind the Wheel in Africa" was distributed by International dealers.*

The Equatorial Heart of Darkest Africa

Commander and Mrs. Gatti on their 9th expedition, which is described in "Great Mother Forest" published by Chas. Scribner's Sons.

The trailers and the fleet of International Trucks are loaded on the freighter bound for Africa.

Two streamlined trailers make five-room home on base-camp location.

Three more International Trucks in the Gatti expedition fleet.

Observation-living room, showing library, bar, and the Commander's desk.

One of two luxurious bedrooms. Electric lighting is indirect throughout.

Electric kitchen that would do justice to the Gatti penthouse on Park Avenue.

Bathroom in black tile. Full-length tub and fittings in superb color harmony.

INTERNATIONAL TRUCKS chosen
for COMMANDER GATTI'S
"Jungle Yachts"

THE celebrated explorer, Commander Attilio Gatti, who has spent thirteen years of his life in the African wilderness, is again at the border of the Belgian Congo, outfitted and equipped for the greatest adventure of his career. During the next year, while the Commander and his wife roam over the immense heart of the equatorial jungle, they will center their operations around their "Jungle Yachts."

The nucleus of the Tenth Gatti African Expedition is a de luxe apartment on wheels—two streamlined trailer units designed by Count Alexis de Sakhnoffsky and powered by International Trucks. Other Internationals will serve the complex needs of the project over an area one-third as large as the United States, and largely unexplored.

Commander Gatti says about his fleet of International Trucks:

"... On our automotive power hangs the success of our venture in the jungle trails and mountains of Africa. We had to have as power cars the very, very best on the market. And we had to have other reliable trucks to carry our great stock of supplies and provisions, our precious movie and photo equipment, our camp, etc. We could not risk the irreplaceable results of months of hard work.

"For this, however, we did not have to make any new research. The many years I have spent in Africa and the 100,000 miles I have already made there with trucks and cars of a dozen different makes have taught me enough. Without hesitation I let experience decide and I took all International Trucks. I know they will give us great service for the major transport and as liaison units for the various parts of our caravan."

International Harvester will be glad to mail you, on request, an illustrated booklet completely describing this modern expedition into Africa.

INTERNATIONAL HARVESTER COMPANY
(INCORPORATED)
180 North Michigan Avenue   Chicago, Illinois

International Truck sizes range from ¾-ton to powerful 6-wheelers.

INTERNATIONAL TRUCKS

Silver Queen

Hawley Bowlus may have invented the streamlined aluminum trailer, but Wally Byam is the man who made it an icon of mobile America. The Airstream name has become almost generic for a streamline trailer, just as Scotch for adhesive tape, Kleenex for facial tissues, and Windex for window cleaner.

Wallace Byam (1896–1962) was born in Baker, Oregon, and quickly developed a will to survive that served him well. Wally's father abandoned him and his mother when Wally was a baby. Mother and son were taken in and cared for by an assortment of relatives. Young Wally sometimes assisted in their work. One of those jobs entailed building roads and another one required living out of a horse-drawn chuck wagon. These jobs almost certainly contributed to his love of the outdoors. After graduating from high school in Oregon, he went on to college at Stanford, where he received a dual degree in journalism and architectural engineering. Armed with his journalism degree, he found employment at the *Los Angeles Times*. Then in the late 1920s, he published five of his own magazines, one of which was a magazine for do-it-your-

1935 AIRSTREAM TORPEDO

Before Wally Byam bought out the inventory from the bankrupt Bowlus-Teller Company, he sold plans for trailers and built some of his own. Pictured is the oldest known Airstream, a 1935 Airstream Torpedo, and its owner, Dr. H. W. Holman, who built it from plans in Popular Mechanics *magazine. The original trailer was sheathed in Masonite. The aluminum was added at a later date. Photograph ©Milton Newman.*

A TRAILER family, abov
enjoying city convenienc
in a rural setting miles fro
the nearest village. Lef
vacation time has becom
trailer time for thousands o
people today.

selfers. The story goes that he published an article submitted by a contributor about how to build your own trailer.

A short while later, the magazine received a letter from an irritated reader stating that it was impossible to build the trailer using the plans published by the magazine. Byam wanted to find out if that was true, so he used the plans to try to construct the trailer and, sure enough, found that it was indeed impossible to build the trailer. Rather than give up, Byam modified the plans and built a trailer of his own design. He liked the result so much that he drew up his own set of plans and published an abbreviated set of them in *Popular Mechanics* magazine. People wrote to him to purchase the complete set of plans and, more importantly, a number of people wanted to buy completed trailers. He found that there were enough requests for him to abandon his magazine business and go full time into the business of manufacturing trailers.

Wally Byam's early models were "canned ham" trailers, so called because of their ovoid shape. These trailers were similar to the English "caravans" that were popular in Europe at the time. Byam sold a number of models of these travel trailers, including the "daring, dashing, debonair" 12-foot Airlite, the 14-foot Torpedo Junior, and the 16-foot Silver Cloud. He also sold the 18-foot Mobile Home that he marketed as "a bungalow on wheels built exclusively to live in." The exterior of the canned-ham trailers was generally plywood, Masonite, or painted Leathercloth, materials not known for their longevity. Byam continued selling plans and building trailers, but the turning point in his career was when he was able to buy the remaining stock and tooling from the bankrupt Bowlus-Teller Company, where he had worked part-time as a salesman.

He formally founded Airstream in 1936. His first trailer, named the Clipper, was essentially the same as the Bowlus Road Chief trailers except for one very important design feature: he moved the door to the starboard side of the trailer. Interestingly, in Byam's autobiographical book, *Trailer Travel Here and Abroad,* which was published in 1960, he makes no mention that his first true streamlined trailers evolved from the Bowlus-Teller trailer. Byam continued to manufacture trailers for a couple of years; but with less than stellar sales and the clouds of war looming, he shut down the Airstream plant and took a job in the aircraft industry for the duration of the war.

After World War II, Wally Byam was hired by a man named Curtis Wright to design a trailer for his company, Curtis Wright Industries. Curtis Wright Industries has no relation to Curtiss-Wright Corporation, a huge manufacturer of aircraft-related equipment. Byam designed a trailer for Curtis Wright and named it the Clipper, the same name as his 1936 trailer. The Curtis Wright Clipper took advantage of some of the technologies developed during World War II, including large wraparound Plexiglas windows. Byam's tenure at Curtis Wright was brief (reports are that he left under less than favorable circumstances), but Byam landed on his feet, and by 1948 Airstream was up and running again. Ironically, for the first few years, the resurrected Airstream company competed with Byam's own design, now being marketed by the Silver Streak Trailer Company.

AIRSTREAM CLIPPER

A magazine article published in January 1937 features an Airstream Clipper. Courtesy Leo and Marlys Keoshian Collection.

The Caravans

Airstream is almost as well known for its Caravans as it is for its trailers. As Byam tells it, one day in 1951 he was visiting with a friend who owned one of Byam's trailers. Byam reports that his friend wasn't getting as much enjoyment out of his trailer as he wished, so Byam suggested they take a trip to Ensenada, Mexico, in their trailers. They had so much fun on the trip that they decided to do it again, but to a different location. The next trip would be much more ambitious: Panama. Eventually, sixty-three trailers of all makes signed up. The journey is well recounted in Byam's book, *Trailer Travel Here and Abroad,* but suffice it to say, as with all adventures it was filled with joy, disappointment, and peril. The group never made it, but fourteen trailers did make it as far as Managua, Nicaragua. Despite the hardships—and an inner vow by Byam that "I would never, as long as I live, have anything to do with a trailer caravan again!"—another caravan took off for Mexico nine months later. Caravans became part of the Airstream mystique and a great way for Byam to showcase his trailers. In 1955 the caravans were formally organized as the Wally Byam Caravan Club International (WBCCI). From the first sojourn to Mexico to Byam's death in 1962, there were two dozen caravans all over the world, the most notable being the eighteen-month Capetown-to-Cairo caravan in 1959–60. During these caravans, Byam was in his element, extolling the virtues of the mobile lifestyle and entertaining community and world leaders.

Airstream after Wally

After Byam's death from a brain tumor in 1962, it was feared that Airstream would lose its compass. During the early and mid-1960s, Airstream produced a number of trailers, most notably the Bambi, that are highly sought after by collectors today. But it just wasn't the same without Wally, and in December 1967 Airstream was purchased by Beatrice Foods, which introduced vinyl-covered cabinets, shag carpeting, and dark wood-grain interiors in 1972. Worse yet, Beatrice management discontinued the smaller trailers in favor of the more profitable longer trailers aimed at retirees. In July 1979, after disappointing sales, Beatrice sold Airstream to a group of recreational vehicle industry executives operating as Thor Industries.

Airstreams are an opinionated bunch of folks and thanks to the World Wide Web they have a ready forum to post those opinions. One of the more interesting comments comes from Airstreamer Don Reasons of Dallas, Texas: "In the seventies, Beatrice Foods had become the owner. Unfortunately, Beatrice Foods was a FOOD company and NOT a travel trailer company. With no experience in this industry for guidance, several management decisions were made which sacrificed the quality of Wally Byam's legendary trailer. Shoddy construction resulting from new corporate management nearly finished off the Airstream company in the late 1970s. It is sad when the image of a first-class, hand-built product like the Airstream trailer can be tarnished by people who have no clue about the industry or the customers to whom they are producing this rather specialized product! Thankfully, Thor Industries rescued Airstream from the clutches of the cupcake maker and gave it a needed shot of integrity. Its treasured reputation was on the road to recovery."

The road to recovery hasn't been instantaneous. The introduction of the so-called Squarestreams (Airstream's Edsel, see page 82) in the late 1980s almost did the company in. As the new millennium approached, Airstream executives knew they needed to realign themselves with America's changing demographics. In this author's 2003 interview with Tim Champ, the head of marketing at Airstream, Champ stated, "We are looking to break out of our reputation that Airstreams are just for old people. Unfortunately our most visible and vocal customers are members of the WBCCI [Wally Byam Caravan Club International]. They are perceived as a bunch of ex-military guys and frankly they don't contribute much to our bottom line. And the Vintage Airstream folks, well, they don't do anything for us either. At this point we don't need the publicity; everyone knows who we are. We need sales. We want to appeal to the hip twenty-year-olds. Once we get them started with Airstream, we think they will continue buying them."

Airstream's first step towards attracting these hip young buyers was the introduction of the new Bambi, with an interior designed by noted San Francisco architect Christopher Deam in 2001. There can be little doubt that Airstream trailers and, indeed, the Airstream name itself are part of the fabric of America. As the baby boomers fade into the sunset and thousands of their treasured Airstreams come on the market, time will tell if these vintage trailers will be snapped up by a younger audience or if they will molder away awaiting restoration by a future generation.

AIRSTREAM SIGN

Jackson Center, Ohio, proudly announces that it is the home of an American legend. Tourists can contact Airstream to arrange tours of the facility, where they will see the Airstream factory and also some of the old trailers such as "Old Grand-Dad" (a 1937 Clipper) and Wally and Stella Byam's gold anodized trailer moldering away in their outdoor parking lot.

AIRSTREAM CLIPPER

One of Wally Byam's earliest Airstream Clippers was on display at the Third Outing Trailer Show in 1936. Trailer manufacturers often displayed their wares at shows that were held in conjunction with automotive exhibitions. *Courtesy Leo and Marlys Keoshian Collection.*

1936 AIRSTREAM CLIPPER

Patriarch in a long line of classics, this 1936 Airstream Clipper carries the earliest known Airstream serial number and also reveals its close kinship to the pioneering William Hawley Bowlus design it was based upon. Following Bowlus-Teller's closure in 1936, trailer builder and former Bowlus dealer Wally Byam purchased some of the firm's equipment and also lured a number of former Bowlus workers into his employ. The resulting trailer, which Byam marketed under the name Airstream to suggest effortless motion, was an amalgam of leftover Bowlus parts and new parts designed by Byam. The primary change from the Bowlus trailer was the placement of the door, which in Bowlus's trailer was placed above the hitch, to a more convenient position on the right side of the trailer, where it has remained ever since. The tow car is a 1937 V12-powered Lincoln Zephyr. The trailer and car, owned by Vince Martinico/Auburn Trailer Collection, were photographed in Penryn, California.

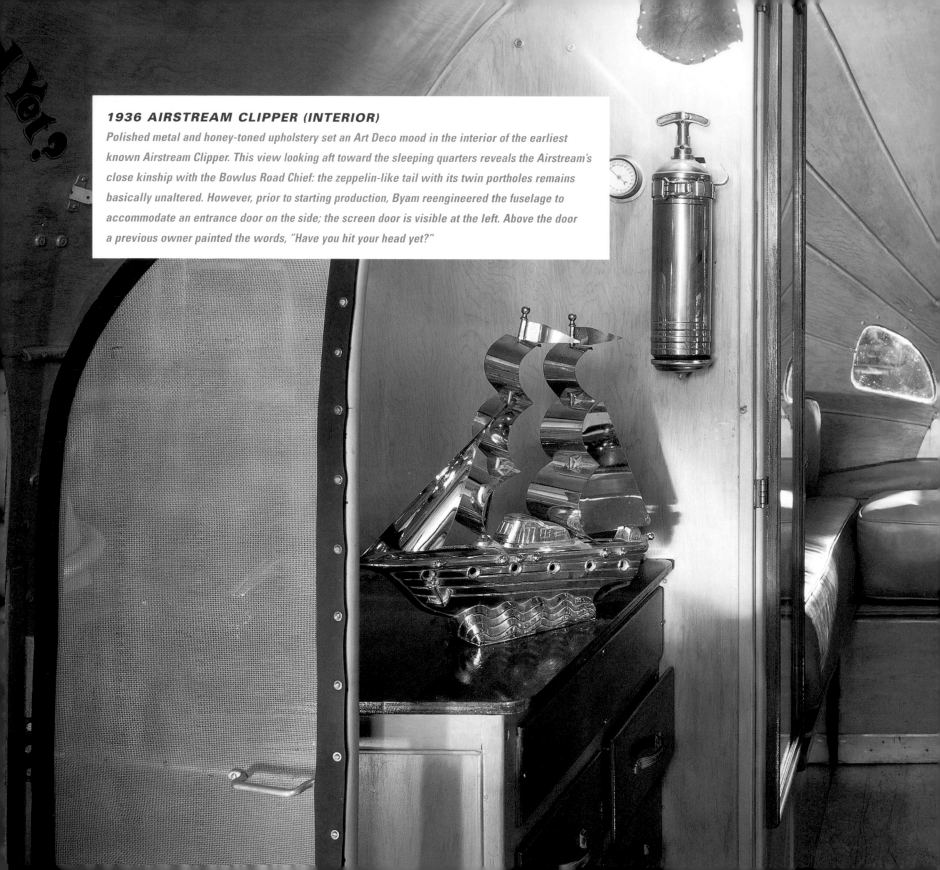

1936 AIRSTREAM CLIPPER (INTERIOR)

Polished metal and honey-toned upholstery set an Art Deco mood in the interior of the earliest known Airstream Clipper. This view looking aft toward the sleeping quarters reveals the Airstream's close kinship with the Bowlus Road Chief: the zeppelin-like tail with its twin portholes remains basically unaltered. However, prior to starting production, Byam reengineered the fuselage to accommodate an entrance door on the side; the screen door is visible at the left. Above the door a previous owner painted the words, "Have you hit your head yet?"

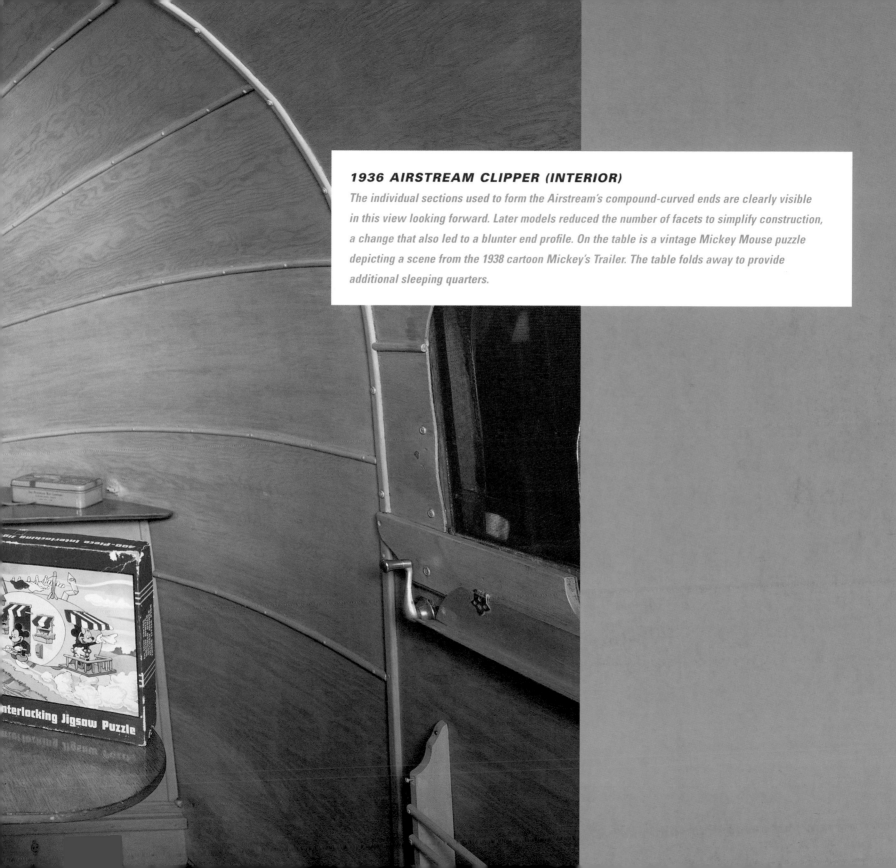

1936 AIRSTREAM CLIPPER (INTERIOR)

The individual sections used to form the Airstream's compound-curved ends are clearly visible in this view looking forward. Later models reduced the number of facets to simplify construction, a change that also led to a blunter end profile. On the table is a vintage Mickey Mouse puzzle depicting a scene from the 1938 cartoon Mickey's Trailer. The table folds away to provide additional sleeping quarters.

1949 AIRSTREAM LINER (INTERIOR)

The interior of the 1949 Southwind is almost totally original, including the propane stove, stainless-steel sink and cabinet, and enameled duro-therm fuel-oil heater. Airstream took great pains to inform its customers that the plans in its sales brochures were merely suggested floor plans. The most interesting modification in this trailer, which was done to provide more living space, was the installation of bunk beds. Treasures from the owners' travels decorate the interior, including her quilting and needlework and a plaque commemorating his tenure as a past president of the Vintage Airstream Club.

1949 AIRSTREAM LINER

The first trailers Wally Byam produced after World War II with the Airstream name were the Liners. The first Liners built in 1947 say "Wallace Manufacturing" on the nameplate. By the fall of 1947 Airstream, marketed as Airstream Liners, was taken over by the McFaul Brothers of Glendale, California. This relationship continued until 1949 when Airstream Trailers Incorporated officially took over the distribution of Airstream trailers. In 1948 Airstream offered four different Liners with various floor plans, from the 16-foot Wee Wind to the 28-foot Whirlwind, known as the Super Duper Colossal Liner. To fully exploit their aerodynamic attributes, other Liners and models were named the Trade Wind, Sea Breeze, Westwind, Zephyr, Chinook, Breeze, and Southwind. The 1949 Southwind Liner pictured here was marketed as the Honeymoon Special model. According to the manufacturer, the 22-foot trailer with 20 feet of livable space tipped the scales at a mere 1,350 pounds unfurnished and approximately 2,000 pounds furnished. The Honeymoon Special was designed to (understandably) sleep two in its "walk-around" double bed. A companion trailer named the Second Honeymoon Special was designed for those who may have lost a bit of their ardor: it had twin beds and a three-piece divan set that could be converted into another bed. In this photograph, to illustrate the streamline style of the trailer, the Southwind is paired up with a 1937 LaSalle Sport Coupe, sometimes erroneously referred to as an Opera Coupe because of its folding jump seats in the rear. The car has a floor shift (the last year, before column shifts became standard equipment) and a hefty 322-cubic-inch flathead V8, which is more than adequate to pull the Southwind. The LaSalle, produced between 1927 and 1940, was the Cadillac's companion car and Harley Earl's styling vanguard. The 1949 Airstream Liner, owned by Forrest and Jeri Bone, and the 1937 LaSalle, owned by Dave Mikol, were photographed at Camp Dearborn, Michigan.

1948 AIRSTREAM WEE WIND

In 1948 Wally Byam was ready to surge forward with Airstream once again as Airstream Trailers Incorporated, which he opened in a small factory near the Metropolitan Airport in Van Nuys, a suburb of Los Angeles. His first product was Airstream Liner, which was essentially the same trailer as the Curtis Wright Clipper and the Silver Streak Clipper. While other trailer manufacturers were looking at building big, bigger, and biggest trailers, Byam saw sales potential for a smaller trailer that was suited for weekend camping rather than an extended stay. The result was the Wee Wind, which used a length-wise spine of tubular steel (seen protruding from beneath the rub rail on the aft end) to support the floor members and ribs. After problems developed with torsional flexing, later units adopted a more conventional ladder-type frame. Airstream marketed a series of Wind models during the late 1940s and into the 1950s, including the Westwind, Southwind, Whirlwind, and Tradewind. At 16 feet, the Wee Wind was the smallest and, thanks to its tubular frame, it was also the lightest (1,200 pounds) Airstream ever made. The 1948 Airstream Wee Wind is towed by a 1955 GMC Pickup with a 350-cubic-inch engine. The trailer and pickup, owned by Ken and Petey Faber, were photographed at Camp Dearborn, Michigan.

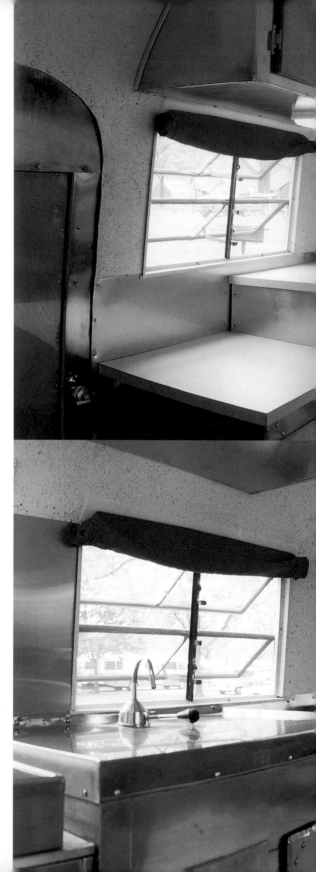

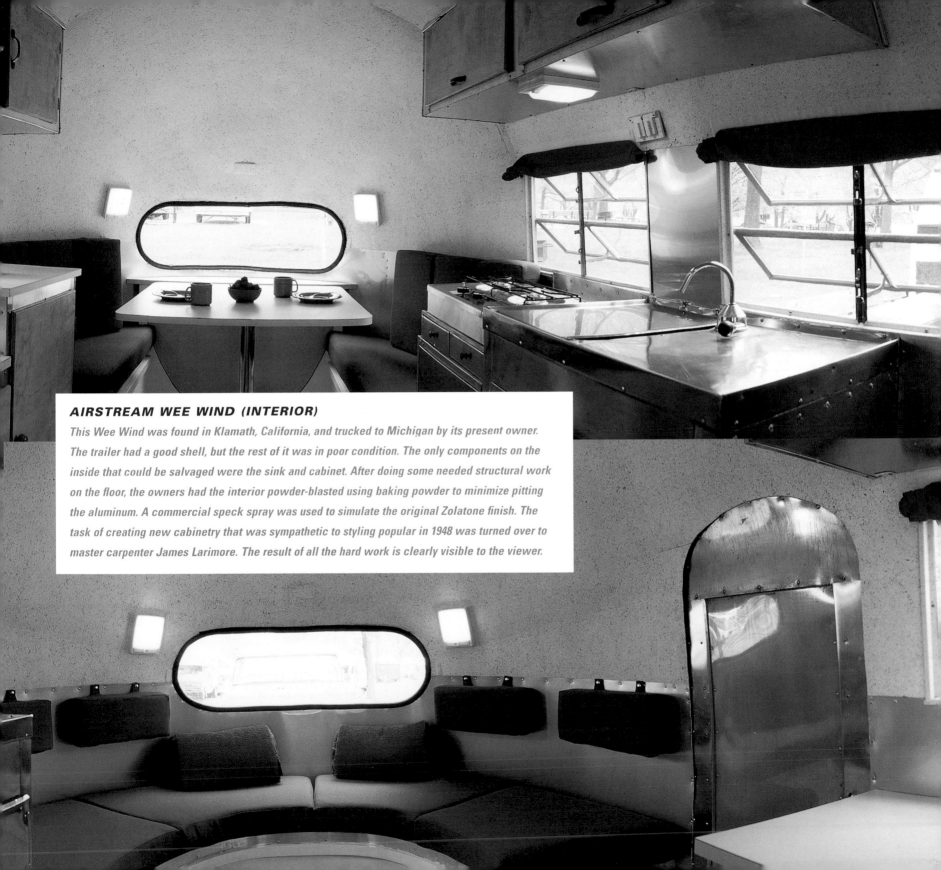

AIRSTREAM WEE WIND (INTERIOR)

This Wee Wind was found in Klamath, California, and trucked to Michigan by its present owner. The trailer had a good shell, but the rest of it was in poor condition. The only components on the inside that could be salvaged were the sink and cabinet. After doing some needed structural work on the floor, the owners had the interior powder-blasted using baking powder to minimize pitting the aluminum. A commercial speck spray was used to simulate the original Zolatone finish. The task of creating new cabinetry that was sympathetic to styling popular in 1948 was turned over to master carpenter James Larimore. The result of all the hard work is clearly visible to the viewer.

1952 CRUISETTE

The 1952 Cruisette pictured here measures just 14 feet 8 inches in length and has the distinction of being the smallest Airstream model ever made. The Cruisettes were only manufactured in the Los Angeles plant in 1951 and 1952 and were targeted to westerners as a backcountry trailer. Less than 100 were manufactured, and only a handful are known to exist. The 1950 Ford Country Squire "woody" station wagon, with its elegant wood-paneled sides and tailgate, exemplifies an automotive tradition held over from the days when station wagon bodies were actually constructed of hardwood. Mike and Noel Conner's Cruisette and Paul and Linda Lyon's Ford woody were photographed at Los Molinos, California.

1953 BUBBLE

The Bubble trailers were manufactured in 1955 at the California plant and in 1956 and 1957 at the California and the Ohio plants. Most of them were configured in a 16-foot size, but some were built and marketed as an 18-footer model. It is a bit hard to track down the lineage of the Bubble because they did not have a nameplate with the Bubble name. The early Bubbles that came out of the California plant are almost as unique as snowflakes, since Byam was getting much of his aluminum as surplus scrap from nearby Northrop Aviation. The size and the configuration of the aluminum skins varied according to what Byam's workers (many of whom were moonlighting from Northrop) had to work with. The interiors of the Bubbles also varied since Byam was not building his own cabinets but was getting them from a nearby cabinet shop. This particular Bubble has a stellar history. Since acquiring it the owner has rented it out for a Beach Boys movie, for a number of music videos, and most recently for the movie Charlie's Angels: Full Throttle. According to its owner, another unique aspect of this Bubble is that it is actually a prototype manufactured in 1953. Ed Carroll's 1953 Bubble was photographed at the Canyon RV Park and Campground, Anaheim, California.

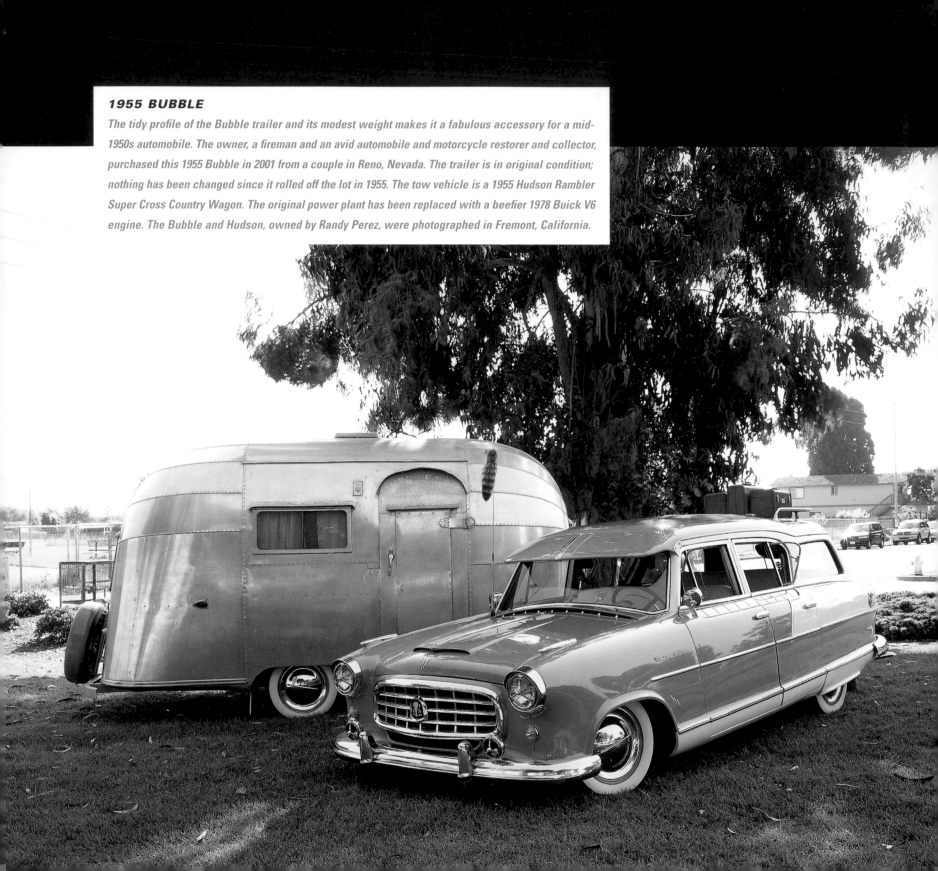

1955 BUBBLE

The tidy profile of the Bubble trailer and its modest weight makes it a fabulous accessory for a mid-1950s automobile. The owner, a fireman and an avid automobile and motorcycle restorer and collector, purchased this 1955 Bubble in 2001 from a couple in Reno, Nevada. The trailer is in original condition; nothing has been changed since it rolled off the lot in 1955. The tow vehicle is a 1955 Hudson Rambler Super Cross Country Wagon. The original power plant has been replaced with a beefier 1978 Buick V6 engine. The Bubble and Hudson, owned by Randy Perez, were photographed in Fremont, California.

1957 CARAVANNER

In 1956 Airstream introduced the 22-foot Caravanner. Light enough to easily tow but large enough for extended excursions, the Caravanner proved to be one of the longest lived Airstreams (it was manufactured from 1956 to 1960 as a 22-foot trailer, then reappeared in 1970 and continued throughout the decade as a 25-foot trailer). The design of the first Caravanner included large windows on the port side. The windows as well as the name Caravanner were a response to the requests from participants of Wally Byam's well-publicized caravans. Linda and Don Coolich's Caravanner was photographed with Duke Waldrop's 1957 Chevrolet Bel Air at the Tropical Palms Resort, Kissimmee, Florida.

1957 CARAVANNER (INTERIOR)

Traveling carnival folks owned the Caravanner and had done some restoration before Don and Linda Coolich purchased it. Linda has decorated the trailer in a Southwest kokopeli motif in shades of plum and gray. The 22-foot trailer is big enough to accommodate a complete bedroom, kitchen, and a bathroom with toilet, shower, and sink. The Caravanner sleeps four.

1957 CARAVANNER

This Caravanner and GMC Stretch Suburban are all ready to set off on an adventure. When the owners bought the trailer in 2002, its condition was just barely good enough to restore. During the seven-month restoration they replaced the window screens, did a number of mechanical repairs, replaced the aluminum skin on the door, then turned over the trailer to a body shop for professional polishing and buffing. The Suburban tow vehicle was originally used by Grey Line Tours to transport people between Reno, Virginia City, and Lake Tahoe, Nevada. Among the vehicle's steady passengers were the cast and crew of the television program Bonanza, who were transported from the Reno airport to the Ponderosa set at Lake Tahoe. Fewer than fifty of the Stretch Suburbans were made. The current owners found it behind a haystack in Yerington, Nevada, then took two years to do the bodywork, upholstery, painting, and finally replacing the hopelessly inadequate 283 engine with a hearty 350-cubic-inch V8. The 1957 Caravanner and 1960 Suburban, owned by Eric and Patty Dobbs, were photographed at the Deming Log Show Grounds, Bellingham, Washington.

1957 CARAVANNER (INTERIOR)

For the interior of their 1957 Caravanner Eric and Patty Dobbs had to start with strengthening the floor, replacing the old flooring with a Pergo floor, rejuvenating the countertops, and finding a new sofa and cabinet over the sofa, both of which had disappeared. After they had readied their canvas for their own personal statement, they chose a flamingo theme. Everywhere the eye looks are the statuesque pink sentinels—lots of 'em: flamingo rug, flamingo glasses, flamingo napkin holder, flamingo salt and pepper shakers, flamingo curtains. If it has flamingos Eric and Patty want it. When they decorate the outside of their trailer the crimson-obsessed pair hauls out a flock of flamingo statues and an assortment of other flamingo-emblazoned outdoor implements.

1964 GLOBE TROTTER

The Bambi may be the most sought after vintage Airstream, but it seems that the Globe Trotter has been the most adaptable Airstream. The Globe Trotter's 19-foot length makes it reasonably easy to tow and navigate and also provides ample interior space to move around and to tailor to the owner's tastes. Arlen and Shirley Manning's 1964 Globe Trotter no doubt takes the crown as the shiniest Airstream on the planet. The owners describe their dedication to the perfect shine as being "aluminumly obsessed." It has been the frequent subject for their polishing demonstrations and has been featured in advertisements and on a television news program. A complete guide to polishing your trailer can be found on their Web site: http://globetrotter64.home.att.net/. Be prepared to spend a lot of hours and a considerable amount of elbow grease. The Manning's Globe Trotter was photographed in Chico, California.

1956 CARAVANNER (SIDE VIEW)

Participants of some of Wally Byam's early caravans suggested that the trailer have more and larger windows. Byam heeded their advice and in 1956 introduced the 22-foot Caravanner.

1964 GLOBE TROTTER (INTERIOR)

The interior of the shiniest Airstream on the planet is clean and efficient. According to the owners, this Globe Trotter's most stellar feature is a modern bathroom complete with bathtub (seen at the left rear). Without a bathroom the owners say that a trailer is "nothing more than an aluminum tent."

1964 GLOBE TROTTER (INTERIOR)

The front of the 1964 Globe Trotter houses an ample dining and worktable that can be conveniently tucked away so the bench seats can be converted into a bed. Combined with the sofa midway in the trailer that can also be transformed into additional sleeping space, four trailerites can be accommodated cozily.

1961 GLOBE TROTTER

*When it comes to trailer restoration, the undis-
puted title goes to Craig Dorsey of Vintage
Vacations. Since 1998 Dorsey, who had previously
worked as an art director, has been bringing
back the luster to these gems of yesteryear. At
any one time he has a dozen vintage trailers at
various stages of restoration in his Anaheim,
California, shop. The most elaborate restoration
and refurbishment for the year 2003 most
assuredly goes to this 19-foot 1961 Globe Trotter
that he restored for Karin Wikstrom-Miller and
Shelby Miller of Santa Fe, New Mexico. Except
for a few pieces of the aluminum skin, very little
is left of the original trailer. The Millers wanted a
trailer that they could take on rugged backcountry
roads, so Dorsey tore off the old axle and replaced
it with a higher-profile axle. He replaced more
than 90 percent of the aluminum skin, changed
the windows, and then added a porthole on the
door, "something that Airstream should have
done years ago." A forty-gallon tank for fresh
water was added as well as tanks for gray and
black water. He also installed an exterior solar
panel, which generates 100 watts of electricity.
With the exterior shell buttoned up and configured, he moved to the inside of the trailer (see
pages 60 and 61). The Miller's Globe Trotter was
photographed at the Canyon RV Park and
Campground, Anaheim, California.*

1961 GLOBE TROTTER (INTERIOR)

Dorsey used 1/8-inch birch plywood for paneling and maple and birch for the cabinets and accents. Behind all of the paneling is a high-tech maze of wiring. The trailer sports three control panels, each with outlets for AC power, 12-volt DC power, cable TV, a phone/modem line, and monster cables for video and audio. In all, Dorsey had to drill seventy-two holes just to thread the wire.

The owners of the trailer told Dorsey that they wanted a queen-size bed, a full kitchen, and a full bath with tub and shower—no mean feat for a 19-foot trailer that, after subtracting 3 feet for the hitch and bumper (trailers are measured from hitch to bumper), provided working space of less than 16 feet long by 7 feet wide. Dorsey removed the bathroom that occupied the entire width of the back, then was able to wedge in the queen-size bed by borrowing some space from the living area and appropriating the space formerly occupied by the bathroom. After establishing the footprint of the bed, he was able to configure the remaining space to accommodate a full working kitchen and a petite bathroom with small sink and a 12-volt marine toilet. But, where to put the tub and shower?

1961 GLOBE TROTTER (BATHTUB)

Dorsey's solution was, to say the least, ingenious. In the area under the seat for the dinette, Dorsey was able to appropriate just enough space to fit in the tub and (with the addition of a spray hose) the shower. If modesty is not required but a stand-up shower is, Dorsey provided an additional hookup for a showerhead on the outside of the trailer.

1964 GLOBE TROTTER (THE EYELUSION MUSEUM)

Looking into the brightly polished surface of an Airstream trailer has often been likened to looking into a fun-house mirror. The undulating aluminum skin of the trailer provides some interesting visual effects. Those effects usually stop when entering the trailer, except in the case of the Eyelusion Museum created by California author C.D. "Doug" Payne. For $450 Payne rescued a 1964 Globe Trotter from the scrap heap, then proceeded to eviscerate the interior, which then became the canvas for his Eyelusion Museum. Payne realized that if he truly wanted a museum that was going to open to the public he would have to provide a way to easily negotiate the exhibits. His solution was to cut an additional door in the trailer so patrons could flow through the displays. Another modification to the trailer was adding a foldout ticket drawer just to the left of the side door. C.D. Payne's 1964 Globe Trotter was photographed in Sebastopol, California.

EYELUSION MUSEUM (FRONT DOOR)

The attractions in the Eyelusion Museum are displayed on pizza pans procured from a local eatery.

EYELUSION MUSEUM (INTERIOR, FRONT ENTRANCE)

Proprietor C.D. "Doug" Payne readies himself to take your donation to tour his incredibly compact fun house. At the center of the photograph is "Wake the Zombie." Patrons are advised to be prepared for a surprise after they pull the lever. To the left of the Zombie is "X-ray Your Head," which creates an illusion known as "Pepper's Ghost." To the right of the Zombie is "Anamorphic Art," where the viewer is invited to turn the handle to see distorted images in the cylindrical mirror. Beyond lie more optical illusions, holograms, and brainteasers guaranteed to befuddle and amaze.

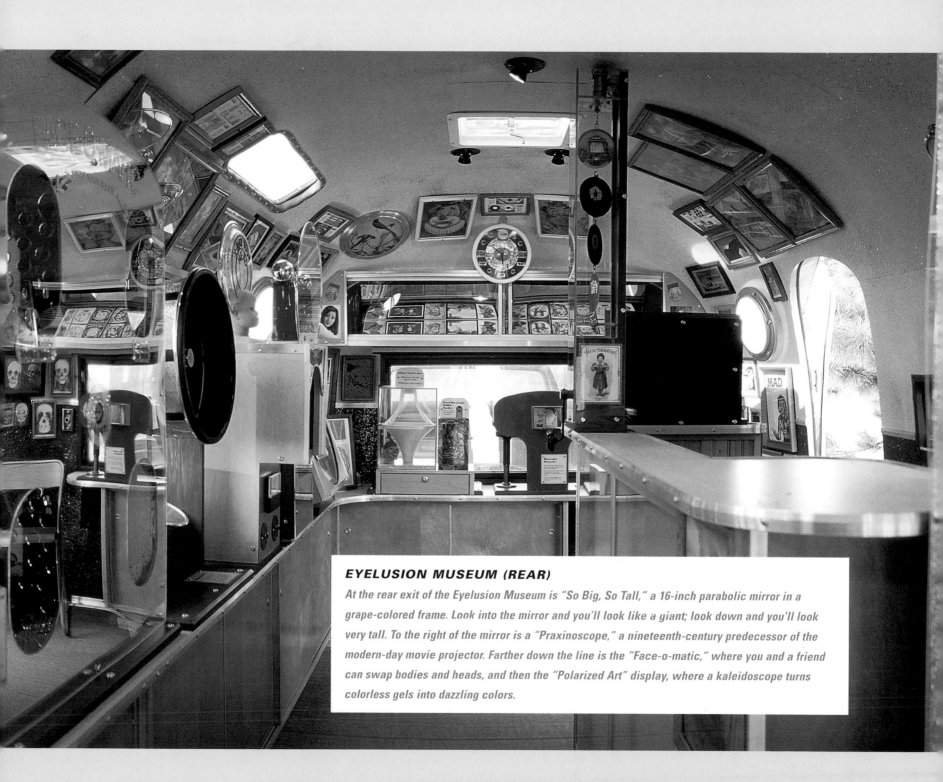

EYELUSION MUSEUM (REAR)

At the rear exit of the Eyelusion Museum is "So Big, So Tall," a 16-inch parabolic mirror in a grape-colored frame. Look into the mirror and you'll look like a giant; look down and you'll look very tall. To the right of the mirror is a "Praxinoscope," a nineteenth-century predecessor of the modern-day movie projector. Farther down the line is the "Face-o-matic," where you and a friend can swap bodies and heads, and then the "Polarized Art" display, where a kaleidoscope turns colorless gels into dazzling colors.

1960 PACER

At 16½ feet and weighing 2,500 pounds, the Pacer was the most diminutive trailer that Airstream manufactured in 1958, 1959, and 1960. In 1961 the Bambi replaced the Pacer. All of these modestly scaled trailers are highly desirable among collectors. The owners of this Pacer, which they call the "Silver Twinkee," spent a lot of time and elbow grease restoring their vintage trailer. During the polishing phase of their restoration they wore out two electric buffers while applying three jars of "Mother's" polish. Dexter and Alicia Leonard's Pacer was photographed at Camp Dearborn, Michigan.

1960 PACER (INTERIOR)

The Pacer's interior (12½ feet long, 7 feet wide, 6½ feet high) has enough room to house a stove, gas refrigerator, sink, double bed, and bathroom. The owners removed the bench seats and table, which originally converted into an additional bed, and replaced them with a 1950s-era dinette set. On the wall at the back of the photograph is a map with highlighted states and Canadian provinces where they have traveled with their Pacer.

1957 SAFARI

Introduced in 1954, the Safari has been one of Airstream's most enduring monikers. The Safari started out as a 22-foot trailer and through the years gradually increased to 23 feet. In recent years, Airstream reintroduced the Safari trailer as part of their Bambi/Safari offerings that they are marketing to young people. This 1957 22-foot Safari is pulled with an elegant 1951 Ford Woody. The owners hand-polished the entire trailer with wheel polish. The trailer and woody, owned by Mike and Kitty Keenan, were photographed at the Canyon RV Park, Anaheim, California.

1957 SAFARI (INTERIOR, AFT SECTION)

The Keenans chose a period-appropriate 1950s theme for the inside of the Safari. In the aft section, the twin beds are covered in a tropically inspired fabric. The binoculars, portable radio, fan, and even the Life *magazine in the rack are from the 1950s.*

1957 SAFARI (INTERIOR, FORE SECTION)

The fore section of the Safari, which contains the galley and dinette, is a 1950s time capsule. From left to right are a pair of horn-rimmed glasses to read the vintage 1957 California road map, brightly colored aluminum tumblers, vintage appliances, cookbooks from 1957, and, finally, a vintage Vargas pinup on the upper right.

◄ 1961 BAMBI

Of all the commonly available Airstreams, none is as desirable as the Bambi. Its diminutive size (16 feet) makes it a breeze to tow and it has all of the necessities (albeit in modest scale) for comfortable camping. Indeed, it is the smallest Airstream to sport a fully equipped bathroom. This particular Bambi, according to its owner, has the earliest known Bambi serial number. There were less than 800 Bambis manufactured between 1961 and 1963. In 1964 Airstream added another 12 inches to the Bambi and rechristened it the Bambi II. The Bambi has a dry weight of less than 2,000 pounds, thus this 1930 4-cylinder Model A Ford is quite capable of towing it. Patrick and Joanne Ewing's Bambi and Model A Ford were photographed at the Deming Log Show Grounds, Bellingham, Washington.

1963 BAMBI ►

The last year of the 16-foot Bambi was 1963, after which it evolved into the 17-foot Bambi II. The owners of this Bambi bought it from a New Holland, Michigan, man in 1989 who had purchased it from an Elkhart, Indiana, Airstream dealer who was going out of business. In the last few years this Bambi has won a number of awards at trailer shows and has been one of the featured stars at automobile shows. The owners consider it their most treasured possession. The Bambi is towed by an age-appropriate 1963 Chevrolet Impala SS boasting a 327 4-barrel engine with a Powerglide transmission that can smoothly tow the wee trailer like a sack of feathers. Ken and Petey Faber's 1963 Bambi and 1963 Chevrolet were photographed at Camp Dearborn, Michigan.

1963 BAMBI (INTERIOR)

The interior of the 16-foot Bambi is actually only 13 feet long since trailers are commonly measured from hitch to bumper. At the rear of the trailer is a combination stove and refrigerator. Right of the stove is a fully functional bathroom complete with shower, configured much like the bathroom on a small boat. Surprisingly, the Bambi will sleep four: the sofa on the right folds down to a double bed and the dinette (out of view, behind) converts into another double bed. Petey Faber, one of the Bambi's owners, is an apt watercolorist and spends much of her time at vintage trailer rallies sketching other participants' trailers.

1963 BAMBI

The Bambi is particularly popular with classic car collectors. Its gentle curves blend well with the automobile styles of the late 1940s through the mid-1950s. This perfectly suited 1947 Mercury woody station wagon owned by Michael and Aedan Haworth tows the Bambi. Both were photographed at the Silver Social, Calistoga, California.

1965 CARAVEL

In 1965 Airstream shuffled its model names again and replaced the shortest trailer in the fleet, the Bambi II, with the 17-foot Caravel. The Caravel's size remained unchanged until 1969 when it was lengthened to 18 feet, where it remained until it was dropped from the fleet after the 1971 model year. The Caravel was the last of the small Airstreams until the Bambi was reintroduced almost thirty years later.

Most of the length variations in Airstream models involved the kitchen and sleeping quarters at the center of the trailer. The forward end on all but the largest units retained the familiar crosswise davenport, which converted into a bed, while the aft end contained the lavatory, toilet, shower, and wardrobe. The 1965 Caravel and 1965 Chevrolet Malibu convertible, owned by Norm and Ann Markus, were photographed above the Carquinez Straits, Crockett, California.

1967 CARAVEL (INTERIOR)

Despite some minor updating with lighter-colored woods and a few plastic panels, the basic interior appointments of the Caravel vary little from earlier postwar trailers. With the increasing use of molded plastic, laminated plastic, and fiberglass panels during the 1970s, however, trailer interiors began to look more like vehicles than homes. The Caravel, owned by Nadine and Jon Yarlott, was photographed at the Deming Log Show Grounds, Bellingham, Washington.

1976 SOVEREIGN

Despite the gas crisis during the 1970s, huge self-propelled motor homes with powerful gas-guzzling engines came into their own. These lumbering behemoths offered amenities like television and air-conditioning as standard equipment and they were easier to negotiate on the roadways and in campgrounds than trailers. Trailer manufacturers were forced to scramble to compete with motor homes. Airstream's answer was to make larger, even harder to maneuver trailers, but with all of the modern conveniences and AC generators to power them. Unfortunately this added considerable weight, and few vehicles were equipped to easily tow these large trailers. It's fairly common to see vintage trailers of the 1950s and '60s pulled with age-appropriate vehicles, it is quite uncommon to see 1970s-era trailers pulled with a vehicle of the same vintage. Thus, this combination of a 31-foot 1976 Sovereign and a 1977 GMC Suburban Classic is a rarity. The Sovereign and Suburban, owned by Tom and Patsy Moreland, were photographed at the Deming Log Show Grounds, Bellingham, Washington.

1976 SOVEREIGN (INTERIOR)

With its molded plastic panels, overhead storage bins, and integrated, ceiling-mounted lighting and ventilation housing, the Sovereign's interior was clearly inspired by the passenger cabin of contemporary jet aircraft. The Boeing 747, the very symbol of modernity at the time of its introduction in 1975, no doubt inspired Airstream engineers searching for a fresh aesthetic.

1989 SQUARESTREAM

If a company has been around long enough, sooner or later it will have its Edsel or New Coke. For Airstream, that moment lasted throughout the 1989 to 1991 model years. Since the mid-1960s, other manufacturers slowly abandoned the ovoid shapes of travel trailers and adopted a more space efficient and economical boxy design. Heeding the words of its founder, Wally Byam— "Let's not change things; only improve them"— Airstream kept its signature shape. Then, some genius at the company decided to change the one thing that truly separated Airstream from its competitors: its shape. The resultant new form was almost universally panned, and soon after its introduction, it was dubbed "Squarestream" by its critics. Functionally, this new breed of Airstreams was little different than its predecessors or other trailers on the market. But in the world of design, perception is the most important element, and the public's perception of the Squarestream was that the company was cutting corners and had become a slave to the proverbial bottom dollar. Kris and Donna Hylton's 1989 29-foot twin-bed Squarestream Land Yacht was photographed at the Deming Log Show grounds in Bellingham, Washington.

2001 BAMBI

As the twentieth century drew to a close, Airstream looked for ways to increase its customer base. Thus, Airstream looked to its past and the Airstream Bambi, which was originally manufactured from 1961 to 1963, was reintroduced, apparently with great success. There are two basic configurations of the Bambi: one is a standard model called the Safari Bambi; the other is the CCD, which has a high-tech interior designed by San Francisco architect Christopher Deam. Michael and Cathy Ashford's 2001 Bambi is shown here with Wayne Fossum's 1933 Ford. Both were photographed at the Deming Log Show Grounds, Bellingham, Washington.

2001 BAMBI (INTERIOR)

Michael and Cathy Ashford didn't think much of the Bambi's interior, so their first step was to do some major remodeling. Michael is one of the luminaries in Arts & Crafts lighting, so he decided to change most of the interior surfaces of the Bambi to make it more sympathetic to the bungalow aesthetic. The couple installed new cabinet doors, countertops, and counter edging; added a new table and sink; discarded the factory fabric and replaced it with something more to their liking. They also tore up the floor and replaced it with teak and Alaskan yellow cedar. A Vesuviana espresso maker bought on eBay completes the intimate scene. After taking out all the old parts, Ashford offered them to Airstream and the dealer, but neither accepted the offer.

Silver Sisters

The early days of streamlined trailers were not unlike a bunch of guys getting together on weekends to build hot rods. Ideas, as well as parts and help, were shared. When Wally Byam acquired the Bowlus inventory in a bankruptcy auction, he had the means and some of the personnel to manufacture trailers of his own design. Interestingly, there were also a couple of trailers that were manufactured in the late 1930s that are essentially identical to Byam's Clipper but bear different names or no name at all. Most notable among these is the 1936 Drayer and Hansen, which looks like a cross between the Bowlus Road Chief and the Airstream Clipper. The Drayer and Hansen has windows like a Bowlus and a side door like the Clipper, but the side door is a double door, which was not introduced by Airstream until after World War II. The Drayer and Hansen also had a toilet (of sorts), which consisted of a toilet seat and a bucket. Another trailer, which also looks like a cross between a Bowlus and an

CURTIS WRIGHT AD

Curtis Wright Industries was the first trailer manufacturer in post-World War II America to roll out a streamlined trailer. The firm had gotten its start manufacturing Homosote-sided trailers in 1944. By 1946, however, Wally Byam had success-fully lobbied Curtis Wright to produce a true streamlined trailer. The result closely resembled Byam's earlier Airstream design and even carried the model name Clipper. The most marked difference was the large Plexiglas windows. The trailer was produced from mid-1946 to mid-1949; however, the iconoclastic Byam had already left Curtis Wright for greener pastures around 1947. This advertisement appeared in the March 1947 issue of Trailer Topics Magazine.

Introducing
A REVOLUTIONARY LUXURY TRAILER...

The CURTIS WRIGHT *Clipper*

Curtis Wright **INDUSTRIES**

TRAILER DIVISION · INCORPORATED
740 VALLEY BOULEVARD
PUENTE, CALIFORNIA

Airstream, is in the collection of Vince Martinico. According to Martinico, this trailer (which does not have a nameplate) was manufactured no later than 1936 and perhaps as early as 1934.

World War II and the rationing of critical war supplies like aluminum put the manufacture of all streamlined trailers for public consumption on hold. There are reports that Wally Byam did make a few trailers during the war, but if he did, they were made for the government or the military.

When the war was over in 1945 and materials and personnel that were needed for trailer manufacturing once again became available, a number of trailer manufacturers geared up for production. Some of these manufacturers had gotten their start in the 1930s, while others were newcomers who saw the potential of selling trailers to the returning GIs. The resurrection of the streamlined trailer belongs not to Airstream but to a curious man with an even more curious name, Curtis Wright.

Mr. Curtis Wright took advantage of his name (which was one S less than huge aircraft manufacturing company Curtiss-Wright) and, no doubt, a sizable portion of his personal wealth and started his own company. Dubbed Curtis Wright Industries' Aircraft & Trailers (the other company was Curtiss-Wright *Corporation*), he manufactured two aircraft in the mid-1940s. In 1945 he manufactured the CW-2 Flymobile, a diminutive helicopter also known as the Wek'copter, and in 1947 he manufactured the CW-21, a small airplane that had a pod-like fuselage and twin tails. But even before the Wek'copter, Wright was manufacturing travel trailers. The earliest known reference to his trailers appears in a July 1946 issue of *Trail-R-News Magazine*. The article, titled "Wright Enters Third Year," includes a description of a Homosote (a siding material for trailers made of pressed paper that is used nowadays as soundboard) trailer that Curtis Wright was making in 1944.

SILVER STREAK AD

This advertisement for Silver Streak dating from the 1960s depicts two happy couples enjoying the great outdoors. Starting in the 1960s, Silver Streak began to use two-tone color schemes by adding panels of gold anodized aluminum. Courtesy Wayne Ferguson Collection.

STREAMLINE AD

This Streamline advertisement dating from the early 1960s, with its woodsy scene of hunters and a pair of eager pointers, stresses the idyllic ambience of trailer travel rather than outlining technical features as was previously common. Billing its product as "The Aristocrat of the Highway," Streamline fielded a full line of trailers. The trailers had slightly squarer lines than the contemporary Airstream but were otherwise quite similar. However, buyers seemingly found little reason to choose an Airstream look-alike over the genuine article, and Streamline remained an also-ran for most of its existence. Courtesy Wayne Ferguson Collection.

STREAMLINE

"The Aristocrat of the Highway"

NEW 18 FOOT SPORTSMAN
For folks who've never towed before

There's a big difference between trailering and Avioning. And this remarkable new model proves it. Hitch it to your present car, power it over freeways or pull it along bumpy back trails . . . we'll wager you'll check your mirror often to believe you're towing a travel trailer. We think you'll marvel too at the space, comfort and convenience in this 3-sleeper. It features a three-burner range with oven . . . choice of roomy 4 cubic foot gas or electric refrigerator . . . complete bath with shower and wash basin.

Another important point, too: This is a full-fledged Avion in every respect. The same riveted anodized aluminum construction—featherlight, maintenance-free, Lifetime Guaranteed. The same well-known exclusive features such as combination screen and door, and bumper-waste hose carrier . . . same as in longer Avion models. And you can choose from a flock of self-contained optional extras.

So if you're thinking BIG quality but small size, consider Avioning in our new Sportsman. Just take another look at the trim lines and practical length in the photo above. Worth looking into a bit further, wouldn't you say? Send for free catalog and name of your nearest dealer. Dept. J, Benton Harbor, Michigan.

AVION
COACH CORPORATION

See the new Avions, National Mobile Home and Travel Trailer Show, Louisville, Ky., Jan. 18 & 19, Aisle TD South, Spaces 2-18.
CIRCLE 50 IN LITERATURE LIBRARY

Although the record is a bit sketchy, it appears that Curtis Wright hired Wally Byam to design its first aluminum trailer. That trailer, named the Clipper (the same name Byam gave his Airstream trailers in 1936), debuted in 1947. Apparently, Curtis Wright's fascination with all things streamlined ended soon after the introduction of the Curtis Wright Clipper, for there is no record of Curtis Wright airplanes or trailers or even the person after 1949. Wally Byam only stayed with Curtis Wright a year or so, and by 1948 he had resurrected his Airstream brand and resumed business as Airstream Trailers.

In 1949 Curtis Wright sold his trailer business to three investors: Kenny Neptune, Frank Polido, and Pat Patterson. These investors opened a business in El Monte, California, as the Silver Streak Trailer Company. Their first model, the Clipper, is essentially the same trailer as the Curtis Wright Clipper. Neptune and Polido, both of whom had previously worked in the aircraft industry, eventually bought out Patterson. Patterson then went on to found the Streamline Trailer Company. Silver Streak continued making trailers until 1997. Silver Streak never made more than a few hundred trailers a year, and by the 1990s most of the trailers were cus-

tom made by general manager Rolf Zushlag, who was hired away from Airstream in 1978. He will unabashedly tell anyone who cares to listen that the Silver Streak trailers made under his direction were far superior to the Airstreams of that era.

Another major player in the streamlined trailer business was the appropriately named Streamline Trailer Company, which was formed by Pat Patterson after his departure from Silver Streak. The earliest documented Streamline trailers were made in 1958, but the company was probably started in 1957. At first it appears that Streamline was not ready to give its trailers any model names; trailers were simply identified by their length. But it wasn't long before Streamline developed a series of regal model monikers. By the early 1960s, Streamline trailers had acquired a royal lineage, from the 19-foot Prince to the 33½-foot Emperor. In between the Prince and the Emperor and ascending about 2 feet with each model were the Princess, Duchess, Duke, Countess, Empress, Sultan, and Count. By 1970 the model names had been changed to the Regency, Imperial, and Crown. Alas, the royal line ended when Streamline went out of business in 1974, but devotees of Streamlines continue to

wave the Streamline banner through the club, the Streamline Royal Rovers.

The trailer company that dared most to go head to head with Airstream was the Avion Coach Corporation. Two brothers named Loren and Robert Cayo, who were both in a manufacturing business, and their friends Allen Grams and Larry Zuhl, who were building contractors, founded Avion in 1955. Loren, Allen, and Larry were frequent campers, and it was their vision to build a streamlined trailer that could be used with full hookups or be fully self-contained when needed. The Avion trailers in their streamlined silver version were made until the 1990s, when the company was sold to trailer giant Fleetwood, which continues to manufacture Avion trailers but in a different configuration.

In 1961 Avion organized the Avion Travelcade Club that was based on the same principles as the Airstream Caravan Club. In 1975 the club declared its independence from the Avion Coach Corporation and continues to have travelcades and hold trailer rallies, which it calls a Rendezvous.

1936 DRAYER AND HANSEN

In 1936 a very curious streamlined trailer appeared on the scene. Little is known about the 20-foot (17-foot 6-inch body) Drayer and Hansen, except that their trailers were a hybrid mix of the Bowlus Road Chief and the Airstream Clipper. It is quite possible that the Drayer and Hansen preceded the Airstream Clipper, since the Drayer and Hansen has all Bowlus windows and, thus, may have been manufactured from surplus Bowlus inventory. It also has a side door, which was an Airstream feature, but the Drayer and Hansen has a double door (one with a screen), a feature that Airstream didn't adopt until after World War II. Regardless of the sketchy provenance of the Drayer and Hansen, it is obvious that skilled craftsmen made it. The most notable feature that separates it from the Airstream is the double compound curves of the aluminum in the fore and aft sections. Airstream engineers either could not do this or it was too costly so they chose to use numerous skins (panels) of aluminum to form the curves. The use of multiple skins give the Airstream trailers their distinctive look but also increases the potential for leaks. Like most trailers of the 1930s the Drayer and Hansen used a number of automobile parts rather than manufacture their own. The classiest parts on this trailer are the Pierce-Arrow wheels. The trailer is owned by Vince Martinico/Auburn Trailer Collection.

1936 DRAYER AND HANSEN (INTERIOR)

The Drayer and Hansen has an all-aluminum kitchen with a sink similar to those found in railroad cars and a rather substantial cookstove. Refrigeration was accomplished with an icebox. Unlike some cheaper trailers, the Drayer and Hansen has double-wall insulation. The top layer was aluminum, Homosote was used for insulation, and the interior was a semi-rigid paneling similar to modern-day Formica.

1936 DRAYER AND HANSEN (INTERIOR)

Many trailers of the 1930s touted toilets as an add-on option, but, in reality, few trailers were actually supplied with toilets and most campers used a bathhouse in a campground. Nevertheless, when you gotta go, you gotta go, and this particular Drayer and Hansen did provide a toilet for those times. It simply consisted of a bucket and a seat, but it was enclosed in its own room. Toilets did not appear in travel trailers to any great extent until the mid-1950s. Holding tanks were virtually unknown, interestingly, because of some archaic laws that forbade the transportation of sewage across state lines. Railroads, which frequently crossed state lines, solved that problem by disposing of sewage directly on the railroad ties while the train was in motion.

1936 AIRSTREAM LOOK-ALIKE

This trailer, found in 2003 in Montana by trailer collector Vince Martinico/Auburn Trailer Collection, was built circa 1936. The trailer had served as a home to a prospector. It has similar lines and features as the Bowlus and Airstream trailers of the same era. Clues such as a maker's mark or patents and serial numbers as well as the trailer's provenance will, no doubt, be revealed when the trailer is fully restored.

1936 AIRSTREAM LOOK-ALIKE (INTERIOR)

In the interior of the Airstream look-alike is a unique keyhole passageway that connects the dining area in the front with the sleeping area aft. The keyhole passageway contains the galley, which houses a stove and sink on the right side and cabinets and an icebox on the left.

1947 CURTIS WRIGHT

Looking suitably Airstreamesque, this 1947 Curtis Wright represents the middle phase of Wally Byam's peripatetic career. Byam's design grew more oblong during his brief tenure at Curtis Wright, and would continue to do so after he resumed production of Airstream trailers. The trailer's larger front and rear windows were of Plexiglas, a material widely used for aircraft gun turrets during the war. At 34 inches wide, the airplane-type door was also much larger than that of early Airstreams. In addition to the 22-foot Clipper, which weighed less than 1,500 pounds, Curtis Wright also offered 16-, 27-, and 31-foot models. The tow vehicle pictured is a 1958 Chevrolet Brookwood station wagon. The trailer and car, owned by Chris and Patti Huotari, were photographed at Camp Dearborn, Michigan.

1947 CURTIS WRIGHT (INTERIOR)

The interior of the Curtis Wright featured an unusual galley located in the prow-like forward end, where it was generously lit by large, curved Plexiglas windows. The interior furniture was demountable, and the trailer could be ordered unfurnished for specialized commercial uses—an apparent attempt by Curtis-Wright Industries to broaden its market appeal.

1952 SILVER STREAK CLIPPER

During the first few years after Silver Streak bought out Curtis Wright, their models changed little. Indeed they were virtually the same trailer that Wally Byam designed for Curtis Wright in 1947. Now that Byam was manufacturing trailers under the Airstream name, it was ironic that he was competing with his own design. This 22-foot 1952 Clipper is pulled by a 1949 Chevrolet five-window cab. The truck has an original Firestone Car Cooler. Just add a little ice and the propulsion of the vehicle activates a fan, thus providing a refreshing, cool breeze-well, for the passenger anyway. The Silver Streak and Chevrolet, owned by Phyllis and John Green, were photographed at the Silver Social in Calistoga, California.

1952 SILVER STREAK CLIPPER (INTERIOR)

The owner of the 1952 Silver Streak Clipper has gone to great lengths to restore it to like-new condition. All of the appliances are sympathetic to the original décor. Ceilings in the Silver Streaks were done in a Zolatone finish. Nowadays, restorers sometimes use Aqua Flex (a multicolor paint similar to Zolatone), though Zolatone is still being manufactured.

SILVER STREAK CLIPPER

One of the features of the Silver Streak, as well as other streamlined trailers in the late 1940s and early 1950s, was the use of Plexiglas to create wide curved windows. Manufacturers touted the advantages of these large windows fore and aft, pointing to the fact that they created a see-through trailer, a definite advantage for a driver, especially when backing up or changing lanes. Like almost all trailers of this size and smaller, the Clipper had a dinette in the front that converted into an extra bed. To make the dinette area in this trailer more like a living room, the owners reconfigured the seating and it no longer converts into a bed. They reduced the size of the dinette table to a size that is more like a coffee table. For more formal dining, the coffee table pops out and a larger dining table is inserted.

1964 SILVER STREAK

Starting in the mid-1950s automobile manufacturers started adopting two-tone paint schemes. Within a few years, Silver Streak followed suit, but instead of a painted finish, Silver Streak used gold anodized aluminum for the accent color. Its present owners purchased this 1964 Silver Streak 22-foot Sabre model in 2002 for $3,500. It is in original condition (complete with electric brakes) and only requires a few cosmetic refinements to bring it back to like-new condition. The trailer, owned by Andrew Broomhead and Lisa Meyers, was photographed at the Canyon RV Park in Anaheim, California.

1964 SILVER STREAK (INTERIOR)

The interior of the 1964 Silver Streak is completely original. In the aft section is a full bathroom with shower and small tub. In the center of the trailer are twin beds that recline to double as lounges. Next to the lounges are 12- and 115-volt lights that are placed conveniently side by side. Out of view is a galley with a double sink and a three-burner stove. In the fore section is a dinette that converts into another bed. Even the curtains are original.

1958 STREAMLINE

The first official year for Streamline trailers was 1958, though some may have been manufactured in 1957. This is a 27-foot two-door "park" model. Park refers to the fact that the trailer has no holding tanks and therefore must be parked in a formal trailer park or campground with full hookups. The present owners acquired the trailer in November 2000 in Iowa and towed it back to California, where they did a full restoration. The tow vehicle is a 1938 Reo COE (cab over engine) Forestry crew cab that sits on a 1978 one-ton Chevy chassis and is powered by 395-cubic-inch small-block engine. The spiffy folding wooden camp chairs were sold under the Leg-o-matic brand. The Streamline and Reo, owned by Chuck and Toni Miltenberger, were photographed at the Canyon RV Park, Anaheim, California.

1958 STREAMLINE (INTERIOR)

For the interior of their Streamline, the Miltenbergers choose a Route 66 theme consisting of memorabilia they have picked up during their travels at diners, motels, and gift shops. They kept much of the original interior, including the aqua paint, fiberglass light fixtures, wood cupboard doors and cabinets, toilet, sinks, shower, and mirrors. A unique feature of the Streamline, which is essential for the dapper camper, is the handy ironing board that is placed in the slot usually occupied by the breadboard.

1965 STREAMLINE DUCHESS

By the 1960s Streamline was well into their regal monikers. This 22-foot Duchess model is one of their smaller trailers. The owner of the trailer is recognized as one of the country's most knowledgeable experts of Streamline trailer history and maintains an archive of Streamline information on his Web site: www.tompatterson.com. The Streamline Duchess, owned by Tom and Marilyn Patterson, was photographed at the Silver Social, Calistoga, California.

Silver Cousins

With the appropriation of raw materials such as aluminum and steel during World War II, the production of aluminum trailers was essentially halted. To be sure, trailers were still being manufactured during the war, but most of them were made of plywood, Masonite, or Homesote (a pressed paper product also known as Beaver Board)—materials not known for their durability and longevity. Many of these trailers were "committee trailers," so called because they were designed by a committee of trailer manufacturers to provide temporary housing to military personnel and workers in supporting industries.

But the new prosperity that followed the war, plus the renewed flow of raw materials to nonessential industries, fueled another boom in the trailer industry. With a decreased need for military aircraft, companies such as Getty Aircraft of Tulsa Oklahoma turned large portions of their airplane manufacturing plants into trailer

SILVER LODGER AD

With the return of a ready supply of aluminum after World War II, manufacturers touted the fact that their trailers were made of lightweight and easy-to-maintain aluminum. To further illustrate that their trailers were made of aluminum, many manufacturers did not paint them. It wasn't until two-tone paint schemes became a popular motif in mid-1950s automobiles, that large numbers of trailer manufacturers started painting their trailers. Such was the case in this 1947 advertisement for the 16-foot (body) Silver Lodger trailer manufactured by the Main-Line Trailer Coach Company in Los Angeles. Other units manufactured by Main-Line were the 14-foot Silver Lark and the 20-foot Silver Liner.

Go Places in Your SILVER LODGER

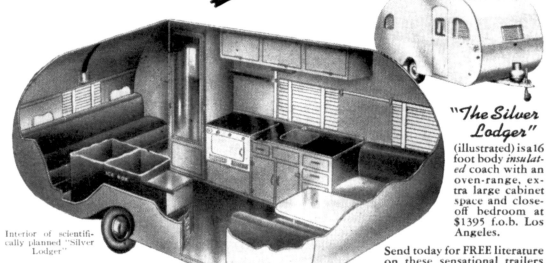

Interior of scientifically planned "Silver Lodger"

"The Silver Lodger"

(illustrated) is a 16 foot body *insulated* coach with an oven-range, extra large cabinet space and close-off bedroom at $1395 f.o.b. Los Angeles.

Send today for FREE literature on these sensational trailers and name of your nearest dealer. Write Dept. "H."

In the mountains . . . at the seashore . . . or by a quiet countryside . . . you're at HOME in a Main-Line *"Silver Lodger"* . . . for a week-end or a year!

This compact, modern travel-home is engineered by trailer experts to assure economy of operation, perfect balance to prevent any swing-sway . . . and *all Main-Line coaches are equipped with electric brakes!*

All trailers sleep four on luxurious innerspring upholstery . . . have a convenient galley to do justice to "homey" meals . . . an icebox of ample proportions.

Main-Line, builders of "America's Greatest Trailer Values," also features "The Silver Lark" with a 14 foot body at $1145 f.o.b. Los Angeles, and the 20 foot "Silver Liner" luxury trailer coach with separate bedroom and "L" kitchen.

STREAMLINE PRODUCTION MAKES MAIN-LINE'S LOW PRICES POSSIBLE

MAIN-LINE TRAILER COACH CO. The Home of the "Silver Lodger"
DEPT. H, 8825 AVALON, LOS ANGELES (3), CALIFORNIA

WRITE ON YOUR LETTERHEAD FOR EASTERN DEALER TERRITORY AVAILABLE.

BOLES AERO '65

QUALITY CRAFTED TRAVEL TRAILERS

manufacturing facilities. Soon Getty was churning out classy aluminum trailers under the brand name Spartan. Sporting names like Manor, Mansion, and Imperial Mansion, most of these trailers crossed the line that divides travel trailers from house trailers. Spartan trailers were manufactured from 1945 to 1959. Spartan did produce one model, the Spartanette, that was marketed as a travel trailer. Spartanettes were produced from 1948 to 1953. The Spartanette and others like it are not true streamlined trailers; rather, they

are classified as "canned hams" because they have the ovoid shape of a can of ham: two flat panels that form the sides and a curving center panel that forms the top and the front and back. By the late 1950s most of the canned hams sported two-tone paint schemes, which imitated the paint styles of the late-1950s automobiles. But in the late 1940s and into the mid-1950s, most of the canned hams were devoid of paint except for accent marks. This lack of paint was probably because the manufacturers wanted it to be obvious that these

canned hams were aluminum trailers and not like the canned hams of the 1930s that were often made of inferior wood products. Once the public got used to the fact that the new canned hams were made out of aluminum, the manufacturers borrowed from the past and again started painting them.

1953 AIRFLOAT

Airfloat trailers emerged in the 1930s. Models during that time were made of wood products and few survive today. Starting in the 1930s Airfloat adopted round windows that give the trailer a definite nautical feel. After World War II, Airfloat switched to more durable aluminum for the exteriors but retained its woody cottage-like interior. This 1953 Navigator model was restored by Phil Noyes and used as a travel trailer. It is now permanently moored in Grass Valley, California, where it serves as Peter and Sarah Arnold's guest house. Elizabeth Mabry poses as a quintessential trailer tart.

1955 AIRFLOAT (INTERIOR)

Perched next to a full-scale compact gas stove is a framed portrait of actress Elizabeth Taylor with her Airfloat trailer. The layout of the trailer follows the postwar standard, with a crosswise davenport at the fore end, a galley, and sleeping quarters aft. Note the unique round-cornered storage hatches above the counter, a clever thematic link to the trailer's porthole windows. The owner of the trailer rents period props to film and television production companies, including the picnic set, ventriloquist's dummy, and menacing cymbal-clanging monkey. The trailer, owned by John Agnew, was photographed at Funky Junk Farms, Los Angeles, California.

1947 AERO FLITE

Built by Aero Lines at the Metropolitan Airport in Van Nuys, California, and appropriately flaunting its "Aircraft Engineered Construction," the Aero Flite amplified the canned-ham styling trends of the late 1940s. Its radically streamlined profile, which seems to belong in outer space rather than on the American highway, featured a bright aluminum finish set off by a highly original hood over the rear window. The 1947 Aero Flite, owned by Kath and Dan Teree, was photographed in Penryn, California.

1962 SHASTA

Shasta trailers are among the most desirable canned-ham trailers. The company got its start in 1941 when Californian Robert Gray made Shasta trailers for military housing. Shasta says the 1941 date makes them the trailer manufacturer with the longest continuous operation (Airstream started in 1936 but ceased manufacturing trailers during World War II); Shastas continue to be manufactured by Coachman in Elkhart, Indiana. One of the most unique features of the Shasta are the little wings affixed to the back of the trailer. Shastas got their wings in 1958, the wings got smaller in the late 1960s when the shape of the trailer got boxier, then the aluminum wings were replaced with plastic; finally the wings were clipped forever when Coachman took over the company. Factory versions of the Shasta trailer are painted, usually in a two-tone theme. But when Luke Hinman, an engineer from Boeing in Seattle, restored this 12-foot 1962 Shasta from the ground up, he just couldn't bear to paint the newly fabricated skin. Patrick Ewing's muscle-bound 1965 Plymouth Sport Fury can easily tow it. Both were photographed at the Deming Log Show Grounds in Bellingham, Washington.

1962 SHASTA (INTERIOR)

Luke Hinman completely restored the interior of his 1962 Shasta. Somehow he managed to shoehorn in a stove, sink, bed, and closet.

1955 BOLES AERO ENSENADA

Another silver contender that went head to head with the Spartanette was the Boles Aero, manufactured in Burbank, California. Like the Spartanette, the Boles Aero falls into the canned-ham trailer classification. Boles Aeros were advertised as "Truly the Aristocrat of Travel Trailers." In 1955 the trailers were available in 19-, 24-, 29-, and 35-foot lengths. Pictured is the 24-foot Ensenada with a full bath. The trailer, owned by Dayton Taylor and Pamela Reeder, was photographed at the Canyon RV Park, Anaheim, California.

Tiki reigns supreme in the interior of the Boles Arrow Ensenada. This style first emerged in mainstream America in the 1950s and reached its zenith in the early 1960s. In the last few years there has been a definite renaissance of the style, especially among young people. A close inspection of the photograph will yield views of Tiki Lounge mugs, an Easter Island tumbler, assorted wiggling hula dancers, a bikini-clad Barbie, and a can of Shasta Tiki Punch.

1960S BOLES AERO

A mid-1960s-era Boles Aero appears to be permanently moored in Toulon, Nevada, just off Interstate 80. The Boles Aero isn't the only travel trailer along this stretch of the Nevada desert that has lost its means of locomotion. Over a century ago, thousands of pioneers trekked across this section of the Emigrant Trail in early trailers (Conestoga wagons) on their way to California. Toulon is located about midway along the dreaded Forty Mile Desert (the longest stretch on the Emigrant Trail without water), and many of the pioneers had to abandon their wagons and possessions just to make it to the next water at Ragtown.

1947 GREAT WESTERN DELUXE

This 1947 Great Western DeLuxe looks like it belongs on a Star Wars *set instead of gliding down the highway. Great Western had a very brief tenure as a trailer manufacturer. In fact, this trailer is the only known survivor of the defunct company. But the company left a stellar, if brief, mark in trailer history. A Great Western trailer (and perhaps the one pictured) was owned by Hollywood star Alan Ladd. Ladd built his reputation by playing tough guys; his most heralded role was as a sensitive gunfighter in* Shane. *He also had memorable roles in* The Carpetbaggers, The Proud Rebel, *and* Citizen Kane. *The role he played for Great Western Trailers was of a vigorous outdoorsman who, "just like Mr. John Ordinary Citizen," liked to take his family to "thinly populated regions."*

Although the Great Western looks a bit bulky, the body is only 15 feet long. According to the manufacturer, the Great Western could sleep six comfortably. How is that possible in a small trailer? That's because four people sleep inside the trailer and two are consigned to the roof, which doubles as a luggage rack. Other amenities of the Great Western include large Lucite windows, a stainless-steel-and-aluminum U-shaped galley, a chemical toilet, an icebox, and a butane stove. The Great Western Trailer, owned by Vince Martinico/Auburn Trailer Collection, was photographed in Newcastle, California.

HOMEBUILT TRAILER

This whale-like trailer was built by an employee at Hughes aircraft in Southern California starting in 1941 and continuing throughout World War II until it was finally registered after the end of the war. The manufacture of trailers like this would have normally been halted during World War II, when defense-related industries scooped up all of the aluminum, but former (and now retired) employees say that quite a few sheets of aluminum, as well as other materials, made it out the backdoor of Hughes. At 25 feet, it is at the limit of a true travel trailer. Despite its size, the leviathan tows remarkably easy, thanks to a clever two-wheeled hydraulically assisted dolly-like arrangement in the front, which is actually a strut from a B-29 bomber (apparently another part that went out the backdoor of Hughes). The strut may have made towing a breeze, but backing up . . . well, that's a different matter. This trailer was equipped with a full bathroom, which was very unusual for the time. Other amenities are mahogany paneling and a humpback trunk. The trailer, owned by Vince Martinico/Auburn Trailer Collection, was photographed at Newcastle, California.

1953 KING

This 18-foot 1953 King trailer, manufactured in Torrance, California, has a classic canned-ham profile: flat ovoid sides and a curving midsection that forms the roof as well as the fore and aft planes. This old trailer was acquired with new technology: it was purchased on eBay. Coupled with the King is a 1956 Willys wagon with a woody-like paint scheme. Woodys (with real wood) were popular in the late 1940s and early 1950s, but they were expensive to build and maintain, so manufacturers looked for alternatives that still fit the woody styling. The trailer, owned by Rose Cayard, and the Willys Wagon, owned by Steve Butcher, were photographed at the Canyon RV Park, Anaheim, California.

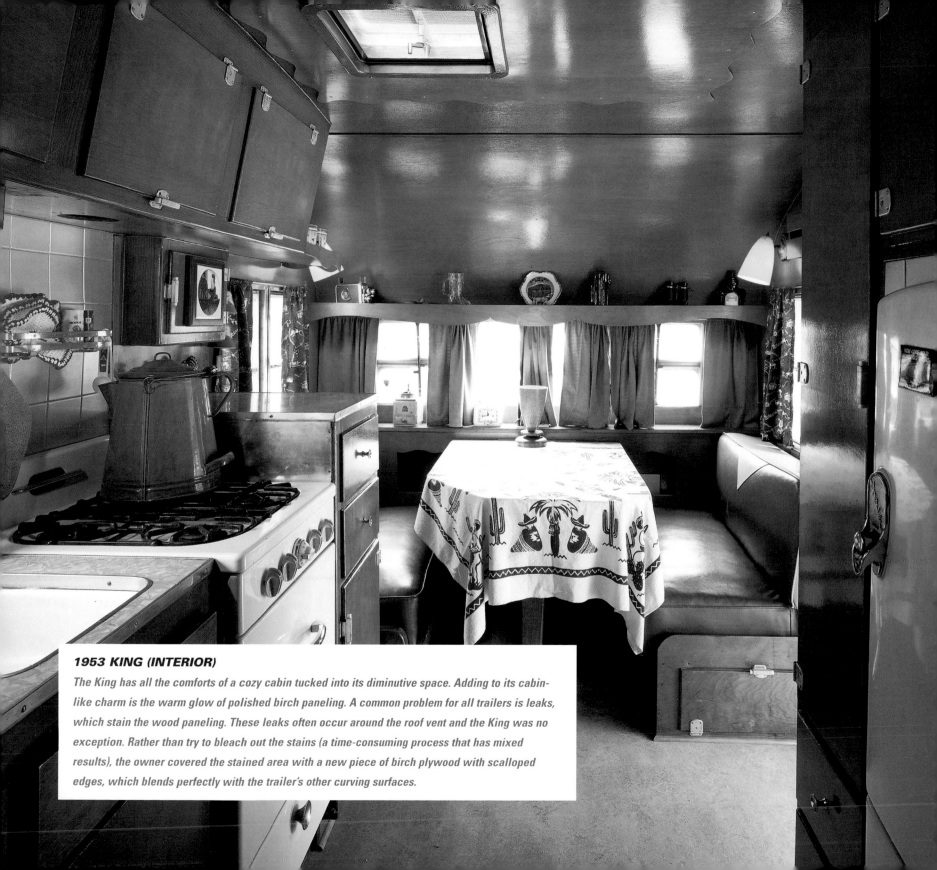

1953 KING (INTERIOR)

The King has all the comforts of a cozy cabin tucked into its diminutive space. Adding to its cabin-like charm is the warm glow of polished birch paneling. A common problem for all trailers is leaks, which stain the wood paneling. These leaks often occur around the roof vent and the King was no exception. Rather than try to bleach out the stains (a time-consuming process that has mixed results), the owner covered the stained area with a new piece of birch plywood with scalloped edges, which blends perfectly with the trailer's other curving surfaces.

1950 SPARTANETTE

The Spartanette was Spartan Aircraft's offering to folks who desired a travel trailer rather than one of Spartan's luxurious but large house trailers. At 28 feet, this 1950 Spartanette pushes the limit of the sort of trailer that can easily be hitched up and maneuvered into a parking space for a weekend getaway. Nevertheless, Spartanette trailers are very desirable within the vintage-trailer community, thanks to their easy-on-the-eye styling and quality construction. The restoration of the trailer was done by Craig Dorsey of Vintage Vacations. The trailer is owned by John and Debbie Crawford.

1950 SPARTANETTE (DINETTE)

After Craig Dorsey did the restoration of the trailer, the Crawfords took on the decorating chores with spectacular results. The birch paneling, combined with the crimson-accented fabrics and gingham curtains, gives the dinette area a warm, rosy glow. The dinette, which easily sits six, converts into an ample queen-size bed. Before retiring, guests are invited to participate in a vintage game of Skip-A-Cross.

1950 SPARTANETTE (GALLEY)

The galley in the Spartanette is located midship, which gives easy access to the bedroom (just visible at the right) and the dining area (out of view, behind the camera). All of the original wood has been painstakingly refinished and the original appliances cleaned and polished to a like-new luster. The red accents on the stove were added to give a punch of color in the kitchen.

1954 TRAVELEZE

Traveleze can trace its roots to 1931 when Kenneth Dixon of Southern California constructed a trailer from parts of a wrecked 1928 Essex automobile, scraps of wood framing, and some plywood. Dixon put a For Sale sign on his creation and it quickly sold. The speed of his first sale convinced Dixon to hang out a shingle as the Traveleze Trailer Company, which sold trailers directly to customers from his Los Angeles factory. During the next few decades, Traveleze expanded its production and was well known as an innovator in the industry. In the late 1940s Traveleze introduced the first gas refrigerator, and in 1948 they introduced the first production motor home by mounting one of their trailers on a truck chassis. Traveleze weathered the crippling times of the 1970s (oil embargoes and soaring interest rates) but eventually went out of business in 1990. RV-industry-giant Thor Industries resurrected the Traveleze brand in 1998.

This 1954 21½-foot Traveleze was found by its current owners in a field on an Indian reservation near Bishop, California. They had previously owned a smaller Traveleze so were well acquainted with the quality of the trailer. The trailer was a "park" model, so in order to convert it to a true travel trailer they needed to add holding tanks for fresh water and gray/black water, as well as 12-volt circuitry in addition to the 120-volt wiring. The owners did a lot of the cosmetics themselves but turned over the wiring and refabrication of some of the exterior panels and doors to Carl Hagen, who they describe as a metal wizard. The paint scheme and the decal design are original. The Traveleze trailer is owned by Susan and Dan Cutright, and the 1955 Chevrolet First Series Advanced Design Pickup is owned by Mike and Debbie Smith. Both were photographed at the Silver Social, Calistoga, California.

1954 TRAVELEZE (INTERIOR)

For the interior of the Traveleze, the Cutrights executed a 1950s cowboy theme and cleverly used vintage bolo ties as curtain tiebacks. The birch wood paneling is original, as are the appliances. The original linoleum floor was in bad condition, but they were able to replace it with reproduction linoleum that is sympathetic to the original design. The backsplash was also in unrestorable condition, so they replaced it with a quilted aluminum panel.

Silver Mansions

Of course, not all RVs are trailers. The other major type of RV is a motor home. The term *motor home* is a rather recent invention. When folks first started converting their vehicles to accommodate sleeping quarters, they generally called them housecars and housetrucks or sometimes they had more fanciful names like motor bungalows. Most of these early motor homes were wood or canvas affairs. Some could be purchased as accessories for a car, but most were of the homebuilt variety. With the advent of Duralumin as a building material, a few adventurous individuals experimented with self-propelled aluminum vehicles and, thankfully, a few of their creations have survived.

HOMEBUILT HOUSECAR

Before the widespread availability of aluminum, housecars and housetrucks were built of wood or fabric materials—with predictably mixed results. Courtesy Milton Newman Collection. The photo was taken in December 1940 by Marion Post Walcott for the Farm Service Administration.

HUNT HOLLYWOOD HOUSECAR

Motion picture cameraman J. Roy Hunt won an Oscar for his camera work on Beau Geste and had a long career behind the lens. His last film was The Juggler with Kirk Douglas, which was released in 1953. Hunt built this vehicle in the late 1940s with the hope of manufacturing many more. That dream never came to pass, but many of his innovations were later incorporated by other manufacturers when motor homes emerged from one-of-a-kind vehicles to mainstream transportation. The main deficiency of the Hunt Hollywood housecar was its woefully inadequate power plant, a 1939 Mercury V8 95-horsepower engine (modern motor homes have at least 300 horsepower). Those 95 ponies were hard pressed to push the 18-foot 2½-ton housecar up any significant grade. The Hunt is owned by Vince Martinico/Auburn Trailer Collection.

HUNT HOLLYWOOD HOUSECAR (INTERIOR)

Despite its small size, the Hunt had ample room for seating and sleeping. Every square inch of space is used, and items like the seats do double duty when they fold down and convert to beds. The entire interior is paneled in birch plywood, stained and varnished to achieve a golden glow.

HUNT HOLLYWOOD HOUSECAR (BATHROOM)

The Hunt even sported a bathroom with shower and toilet. The toilet was, in reality, little more than a bucket with a seat. It would be years before truly functional toilets were available for recreational vehicles.

HUNT HOLLYWOOD HOUSECAR (INTERIOR)

Nowadays, people complain about drivers motoring down the road while talking on cell phones. Imagine seeing someone making coffee, frying eggs, or doing the dishes while driving? All of these things were possible in the Hunt, although they may have been a bit hazardous to the driver as well as to the vehicles he encountered.

THOMPSON HOUSECAR

The Thompson "Raise the Roof Four-Sleeper and Diner Cabin Sedan" looks like a cross between an armored car and a limousine. There were only a few of the Thompsons made and they are, understandably, highly desirable among collectors. The roof raises by an ingenious series of gears that, when properly aligned, raise all four corners of the roof simultaneously. The Thompson was the creation of watchmaker Arthur Thompson of Ontario, California. He constructed the first Thompson in 1934 using a Studebaker chassis powered by a 6-cylinder engine. The Thompson housecar was featured in a 1937 issue of Life magazine and in a 1938 issue of Motor magazine, where it was described as a "caravan car." The Thompson is owned by Vince Martinico/Auburn Trailer Collection.

THOMPSON HOUSECAR

With the roof fully extended, folks could stand upright in the Thompson. Product literature claimed that with the steering wheel folded forward and the seats laid back, four could sleep comfortably. In the galley at the rear are a refrigerator and a sink with running water.

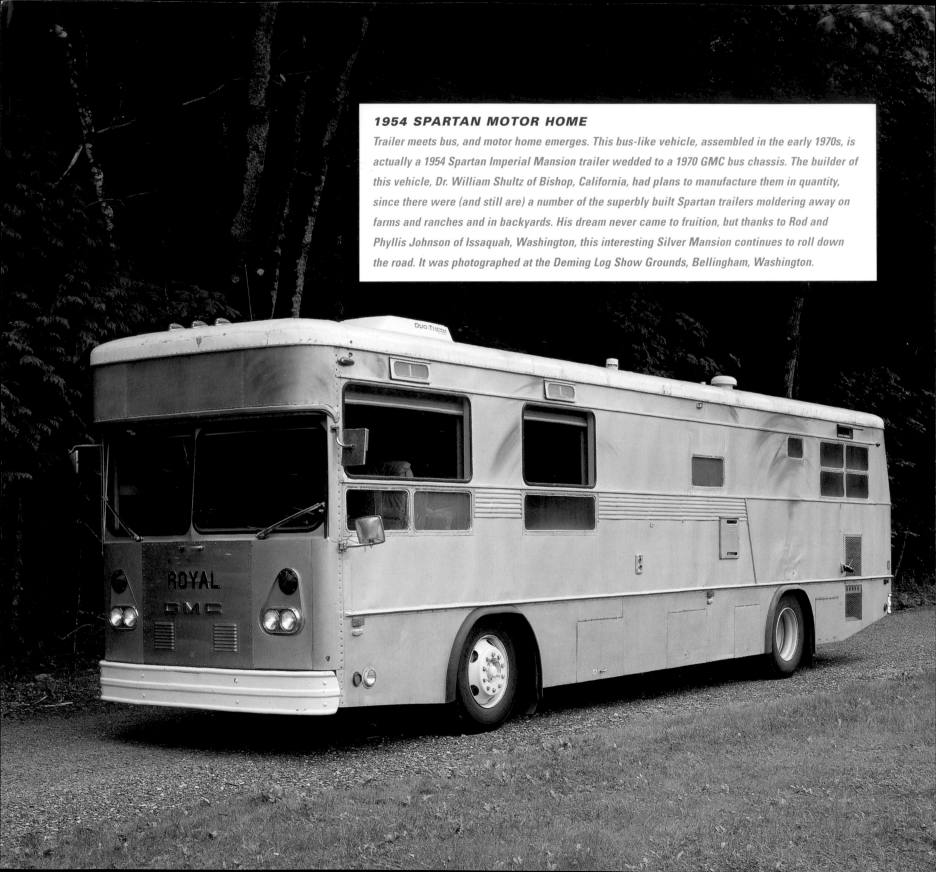

1954 SPARTAN MOTOR HOME

Trailer meets bus, and motor home emerges. This bus-like vehicle, assembled in the early 1970s, is actually a 1954 Spartan Imperial Mansion trailer wedded to a 1970 GMC bus chassis. The builder of this vehicle, Dr. William Shultz of Bishop, California, had plans to manufacture them in quantity, since there were (and still are) a number of the superbly built Spartan trailers moldering away on farms and ranches and in backyards. His dream never came to fruition, but thanks to Rod and Phyllis Johnson of Issaquah, Washington, this interesting Silver Mansion continues to roll down the road. It was photographed at the Deming Log Show Grounds, Bellingham, Washington.

LEGGETTE MOTOR HOME

Evangelist Billy Leggette built this one-of-a-kind motor home in Prince George, British Columbia, Canada, in 1962–63. Leggette's design for his mobile home was apparently divinely inspired. In a flyer he distributed to his flock describing his evangelical mission he says, "God gave me a mental picture of this design and dimensions while waiting before Him in prayer." The truck is a 1962 GMC 930 Five Ton Chassis, powered by a modest 261-cubic-inch inline 6-cylinder engine. Leggette and his wife traveled in their mobile mansion throughout Canada, the USA, and Mexico, spreading the Gospel until his death in 1978 at age sixty-five. The present owner, Bill Coulson, rescued it from a farm property where it had been sitting for seventeen years. It was photographed at Camp Dearborn, Michigan.

Silver Snapshots

Trailerites — and, by extension, owners of motor homes and other RVs — just might be the friendliest people on the planet. The reason why is amazingly simple: they can move at will. Sociologists say that we humans are herd animals; we seek out our own kind. And sooner or later we appoint leaders, sometimes with positive results and sometimes without. The problem we have when we gather together for any length of time is that we often encounter folks who are, well, troublesome. If we are in a bolted-down community, we are understandably a bit skittish about developing relationships with our neighbors, at least until we've lived around them for a while. But mobile Americans are much quicker to develop relationships with their neighbors because they know that if things don't work out, a simple turn of the key in the ignition provides a ready solution.

This friendliness and camaraderie can be seen among the members of the various RV associations, like the Tin Can Tourists (owners of vintage RVs), The Good Sam Club (the nation's largest RV association), and the Escapees (an organization of people who live full-time on the road). There are also a number of organizations that cater to owners of specific RVs, like the Airstream Club, the Shasta Club, the Boler Club, the teardrop clubs, and many others. These people are quick to share ideas, to assist in a chore, or just to lend an ear.

Octogenarian John Culp, who lives full time in a 1947 Westwood trailer that was purchased new by his parents, may best sum up this feeling of fellowship. Says John, "Trailerites just seem to get along. I've been to lots of campgrounds where someone with a half-million-dollar

John Culp and George with his 1947 Westwood Coronado at a Tin Can Tourists Winter Reunion in Kissimmee, Florida.

If you're going to collect something, you might as well show it off. Trailer rallies are the perfect place to show off your collection of . . . well . . . just about anything. People who restore vintage trailers don't stop their collecting and restoring with trailers. They are usually avid antiquers and often collect travel-related items like license plates, maps, period kitchen utensils, tools, and ephemera. This is the tip of the iceberg of Randy Perez's collection of plaid camping accoutrements.

Vintage trailer restorers can't seem to stop with one trailer and they frequently trade trailers amongst themselves. This Great Western trailer (see page 129) was found in a junkyard by trailer collector Jerry Rice, who brought it to the Silver Social trailer rally in Calistoga, California. Kath Teree took a liking to it after checking out the view from the observation deck. Trailer collector extraordinaire Vince Martinico ultimately purchased it from Rice, but not before he sold his Aero Flite trailer (see page 118) to Kath and her husband, Dan.

For many years, Loren and Rhonda Perkins operated the Storie Retreat Bed and Breakfast in Northern California's scenic Feather River Canyon. A few years ago they purchased a battered Airstream trailer and towed it to their property with the long-term goal of restoring it. As soon as they parked the old Airstream they had their guests asking if they could stay in it. Their guests said staying in the trailer brought back memories of past family vacations. In short order, Loren and Rhonda were combing the countryside looking for other silver palaces. They now have eight Airstreams (an assortment of Tradewinds, Safaris, and Overlanders) and a Streamline Countess.

Arlen and Shirley Manning bask in the glow of their 1964 Airstream Globe Trotter (see page 53) in a field of sunflowers in Chico, California.

Prevost Motor Coach will pull in next to someone in a tent trailer. Soon, they'll be talking and maybe even sharing a meal. They have something in common, I guess. A love of the road or maybe just the freedom to move wherever they want." Then with a sly grin and a wink, John will say, "It's not that way with everybody who shares a common passion. The canoe people and the yacht people—they don't really mix much."

In Bisbee, Arizona, a thousand miles or so south of the Storie Retreat, is the Shady Dell, America's premier trailer bed and breakfast. Here, guests can stay in an assortment of immaculately restored silver palaces, including (from right to left) a 1954 Crown, a 1957 El Rey, a 1949 Airstream Honeymoon Special with a polished ceiling, a Spartanette, a Spartan Mansion, and a Spartan Royal Mansion.

Travelers along California's scenic Highway 70 in the Feather River Canyon often do the proverbial double take as they motor on by the Storie Retreat.

The 1953 King trailer may belong to Rose Cayard but Steven Butcher is firmly in control of the remote control. Couples say that restoring vintage trailers and going to trailer rallies is something they seem to enjoy equally. The division of labor is usually quite clear: the men are in charge of the hardware and the women are in charge of the nest.

The intermittently gallant Ed Carroll offers his spouse, Joan, a hand as she exits their 1953 Airstream Bubble.

Karen Wikstrom-Miller, fresh from a soak in their custom tub, chillily poses with her husband, Shelby Miller, in front of their 1961 Airstream Globe Trotter.

Lisa Meyers, Andrew Broomhead, and Kanan with their 1964 Silver Streak at a vintage-trailer rally in Anaheim, California.

Trailer rallies are often places to exchange information about old trailers. One of the more popular topics concerns the polishing of aluminum. At the Silver Social in Calistoga, California, Tom Numelin, who promotes his polishing regime at www.perfectpolish.com, demonstrates the proper buffing technique.

Spokesmodel Annie Neal demonstrates the shine achieved with the proper polishing technique, the largest part being lots of elbow grease.

John Agnew, proprietor of Funky Junk Farms, hitches up at a vintage-trailer rally in Los Angeles. Funky Junk Farms rents vintage trailers and other period props to Hollywood production companies. Find them at www.funkyjunkfarms.com.

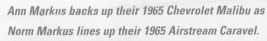

Ann Markus backs up their 1965 Chevrolet Malibu as Norm Markus lines up their 1965 Airstream Caravel.

Mike Smith enjoys a refreshing beverage with Dan and Susan Cutright at their 1954 Traveleze trailer during the Silver Social in Calistoga, California.

Marlys and Leo Keoshian are the proud owners of a rare 1935 Bowlus Papoose.

Luke Hinman reconstructed his 1962 Shasta from the ground up, including the complete refabrication of the aluminum skin, using skills he developed while working at Boeing Aircraft in Seattle.

Aedan and Michael Haworth showed up at the Silver Social in Calistoga, California, with their 1965 Airstream Bambi and 1947 Mercury woody.

Canadians Kevin and Ann Sagert, who travel with a full complement of portable canines in their 1969 Airstream Ambassador, were photographed at the Tin Can Tourists/Vintage Airstream Club rally in Bellingham, Washington.

Trailer rallies are a time to get together to share information, relax with friends, and enjoy the outdoor life (with a silver roof at night). Michael Ashford serves up the steaks at Tin Can Tourists/Vintage Airstream Club rally in Bellingham, Washington.

Ken Faber and his wife, Petey, are avid vintage-vehicle collectors. Here he is pictured with their 1963 Airstream Bambi and their 1963 Chevrolet Impala at the Tin Can Tourists summer reunion in Camp Dearborn, Michigan.

Eric and Patty Dobbs of Snohomish, Washington, have gone to the birds. They have restored a number of vintage trailers. This one, an Airstream Caravanner, is done in a flamingo theme.

Tin Can Tourists members Chuck and Dianne Schneider do not confine their collecting to trailers. They also collect vintage vehicle toys, automobiles, and orchard tractors.

The Tin Can Tourists, an organization that can trace its roots to 1919, is open to people who own an RV that is at least twenty-five years old. Pictured is a lecture about the Ultravan, a Corvair-powered motor home, at a Tin Can Tourists rally in Camp Dearborn, Michigan.

Vintage trailer rallies draw all types of people who come to share information, buy and sell, and mostly to enjoy the company of others who share their passion. Pictured is Patrick Ewing, Tin Can Tourists regional president, addressing the assembled throng at a Tin Can Tourists/Vintage Airstream rally in Bellingham, Washington. The trailer is a vintage Boles Aero.

1963 Airstream
"Get Your Kicks on Route 66"

At any one time, trailer collector extraordinaire Vince Martinico has more than forty trailers on his property, which he calls The Auburn Trailer Collection. Martinico has two barns full of trailers: one barn houses the trailers he is keeping for a future museum; the other barn houses trailers he has for sale.

Resources

Interested in finding out more? Here's a list of Web sites that will help you on your quest. If you don't find exactly what you are looking for, you'll find that most of these Web sites have links to other trailer-related Web sites.

Information on specific trailer brands and types

Airstream: www.vintageairstreamclub.org
All Silver Trailers: www.airstreamsites.com
Avion: www.avionclub.org
Bowlus: home.earthlink.net/~raulb/roadchief.html
Spartan: www.spartantrailer.com
Streamline: www.tompatterson.com

Clubs and Organizations

Airstream: www.vintageairstreamclub.org
Avion Travelcade Club: www.avionclub.org
Good Sam Club: www.goodsamclub.com
Tin Can Tourists: www.tincantourists.com
Wally Byam Caravan Club: www.wbcci.org

Trailer Memorabilia

www.airstreamdreams.com
www.hav-a-look.com

Trailer Sales, Rentals, and Restoration

www.auburntrailercollection.com
www.funkyjunkfarms.com
www.iowaboys.com
www.vintage-vacations.com
www.vintagecampers.com

Museums

Nethercutt Museum: www.nethercuttcollection.org
Petersen Museum: www.petersen.org
RV Museum: www.rv-mh-hall-of-fame.org
Shelburne Museum: www.shelburnemuseum.org

Polishing Techniques

Arlen and Shirley's 1964 Globe Trotter:
    globetrotter64.home.att.net/complete.htm
Perfect Polish: www.perfectpolish.com
The Polishing Centre: www.preairdet.ca/airstream.htm
The Polishing Guru: www.inlandrv.com/polishing

Links

Explore all of the above sites for links. A very comprehensive list can be found on Craig Dorsey's Vintage Vacations site: www.vintage-vacations.com/trailerlinks.htm

Trailer King

Vince Martinico is in a class by himself. He buys, sells, restores, and collects all manner of trailers, trailer memorabilia, and house cars. You can find him on the Internet at www.auburntrailercollection.com or e-mail him at bigyellowt@yahoo.com.

Acknowledgments

The author is very grateful for the time and assistance of the following people:

Duke and Fay Waldrop
Forrest and Jeri Bone
Dan and Linda Coolich
Milton Newman
Vince Martinico
Ken and Petey Faber
John Culp
Bill and Dr Bob
Julie Castiglia
Rick and Janice Meyers
Allan Woods
Dexter and Alicia Leonard
Mark and Rhonda Gelstein
Dave Mikol
Jim and Midge Markus
Norm and Ann Markus
Luke Hinman
Patrick and Joanne Ewing
Mike and Cathy Ashford
Kris and Donna Hylton
Rod and Phyllis Johnson
Tom and Patsy Moreland
Andy and Linda Denham
Eric and Patty Dobbs
Kevin and Ann Sagert
Arlen and Shirley Manning
John and Phyllis Green

Dan and Susan Cutright
Randy Perez and Madeline
Michael and Aeden Haworth
Tom and Marilyn Patterson
Pat and Darcy Porter
Dan and Kath Teree
Mike and Debbie Smith
Chuck and Toni Miltenberger
Shelby Miller and Karin Wikstom-Miller
Mike and Kitty Keenan
Steven Butcher and Rose Cayard
John Agnew
Andrew Broomhead and Lisa Meyers
John and Debbie Crawford
Dayton Taylor and Pamela Reeder
Leo and Marlys Keoshian
Craig Dorsey
Kimberly Steiner
Bob and Marilyn West
Chris and Patti Huotari
Mike and Noel Conner
Paul and Linda Lyon
Ed and Joan Carroll
Chuck and Dianne Schneider
C. D. Payne
Jon and Nadine Yarlott
Loren and Rhonda Perkins
Wayne Fossum
Howard Cohen
Wayne and Kathy Ferguson
Elizabeth Mabry

Skip Marketti
Arrol Gellner
Don and Carol Mayton
Travis Travnikar
Dean Pederson and Sarah Burkdoll
Bill Coulson
Peter and Sarah Arnold
Phil Noyes
Bob Haworth
Buddy the Dog
Goldie the Dog
George the Dog
The Chihuahuas
Shady Dell Bed and Breakfast, Bisbee, Arizona
Canyon RV Park, Anaheim, California
Storie Retreat, Storie, California
The Magazine Archives, San Francisco, California
Tropical Palms Resort, Kissimmee, Florida
Camp Dearborn, Dearborn, Michigan
The Deming Log Show Grounds, Bellingham, Washington
The Tin Can Tourists
The Vintage Airstream Club
Al at the Photo Lab, Chico, California
The Groovy Guys and Gals at Gibbs Smith, Publisher
And especially my wife, Sandra Schweitzer

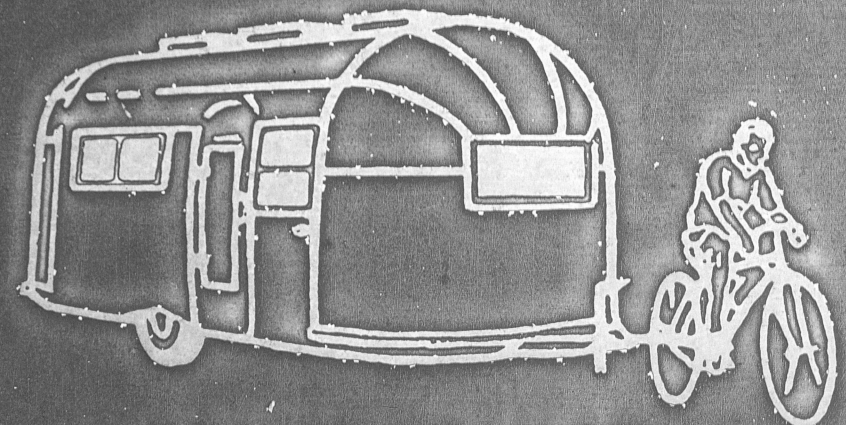

A TRAVEL TRAILER